Spiritual Heart

A compilation of the three most important topics relating to spiritual illnesses and their cures

By
Shaykh Mufti Saiful Islām

JKN Publications

© Copyright by JKN Publications

First Published in December 2015

ISBN 978-1-909114-10-4

British Library Cataloguing in Publication Data
A catalogue record for this book is available from the British Library.

All Rights Reserved. No part of this book may be reproduced, stored in a retrieval system or transmitted in any form or by any means, electronic, mechanical, photocopying, recording or otherwise, without the prior permission of the copyright owner.

Publisher's Note:

Every care and attention has been put into the production of this book. If however, you find any errors, they are our own, for which we seek Allāh's ﷻ forgiveness and the reader's pardon.

Published by:

JKN Publications
118 Manningham Lane
Bradford
West Yorkshire
BD8 7JF
United Kingdom

t: +44 (0) 1274 308 456 | w: www.jkn.org.uk | e: info@jkn.org.uk

Book Title: Spiritual Heart

Author: Shaykh Mufti Saiful Islām

"In the Name of Allāh, the Most Beneficent,
the Most Merciful"

Contents

Pride – The Detrimental Effects of Pride and its Remedies

Introduction 6
An Inspiring Incident 8
Shaykh Muhammad-Ullāh's ﷺ Visit to Shaykh Ashraf Ali Thānwi ﷺ 9
Allāmah Sayyid Sulaimān Nadwi's ﷺ Visit to Shaykh Ashraf Ali Thānwi ﷺ 10
Status of Abū Zar ﷺ 11
The Humility of Our Pious Predecessors 12
The Virtues of Humility 13
An Inspiring Incident 14
What is Takabbur? 15
Qualities of a Spiritual Shaykh 16
A Question Posed to Shaykh Ashraf Ali Thānwi ﷺ 19
A Girl Getting Married 19
The Famous Du'ā of Sayyidunā Ibrāheem ﷺ 20
The Nature of Ujb (Vanity) 22
An Incident of Deep Reflection 22
Cure for Pride 31

Cure for Anger

Introduction 34
The Importance and Rewards for Restraining Anger 35
Sayyidunā Abū Mas'ood ﷺ Hitting his Slave 37
Sayyidunā Abū Bakr Siddique ﷺ Restrains his Anger 39

Zainul-Ābideen ؓ Restrains his Anger 40
Incidents of the Pious Who Restrained Their Anger 41
Damaging Effects of Extreme Anger 45
Allāh's ﷻ Sustenance.. 46
Sayyidunā Mūsā ؑ and the Goat... 47
A Bedouin Urinates in the Masjid 48
Four Types of People Who Become Angry............................. 49
Remedy for Anger 50
Prescription of the Pious 51
Anger Management by Dr Rafāqat Rasheed........................ 53

Protecting the Gaze

Introduction.. 83
Avenues of Sins.. 84
Avenues of Adultery and Fornication..................................... 85
Wisdom Behind the Verses of Sūrah An-Noor....................... 86
First Stage - Protecting the Gaze.. 86
Bounty of Vision.. 87
Reward for Viewing Certain Things.. 88
Spiritual Insight of Sayyidunā Abū Ubaidah ؓ 90
An Amazing Incident.. 92
A Second Amazing Incident... 94
Holy Prophet's ﷺ Compassion with a Young Companion........ 95
Four Avenues of Attack... 97
Harms of Casting Evil Glances... 98
Prescription... 101

5

Introduction

Allāh ﷻ says,

إِنَّهُ لَا يُحِبُّ الْمُسْتَكْبِرِينَ

"Indeed Allāh does not love the proud ones." (16:23)

In another place He states,

وَلَهُ الْكِبْرِيَاءُ فِي السَّمَاوَاتِ وَالْأَرْضِ وَهُوَ الْعَزِيزُ الْحَكِيمُ

To Him belongs the pride in the heavens and the earth and He is the Almighty, the All-Wise. (45:37)

The first verse explains that those who possess even a slight amount of pride in their hearts are deprived of the love of Allāh ﷻ. In the Arabic language, إِنَّ (indeed) comes for emphasis and the verb لَا يُحِبُّ (does not love) is in the present and future tense, implying that Allāh ﷻ does not love the proud and boastful people at present and will continue to dislike them in the future, until the element of pride is eradicated and erased from their hearts. Hence, the Qur'ānic verse informs us that He dislikes those who harbour pride and haughtiness in them.

In the second verse, the letter Lām in 'وَلَهُ' comes for Takhsees – exclusiveness, i.e. highness is exclusive to Allāh ﷻ. In relation to this, there is a Nahw ruling: التقديم ما حقه التأخير يفيد الحصر - "To precede with a word, which according to grammar rules should be brought at the end, renders the benefit of exclusiveness." The Qur'anic verse will thus mean, **To Allāh ﷻ alone does pride belong.** Thus, it is not befitting for anyone else apart from Him. Allāh ﷻ then concludes the verse by proclaiming;

وَهُوَ الْعَزِيزُ الْحَكِيمُ

He is the Almighty, the Most Wise.

Why did Allāh ﷻ reveal these two particular attributes of His out of the numerous other names?

Showing pride stems out for two reasons; firstly, due to extreme power and secondly, knowing how to use this power appropriately with wisdom. Hence Allāh ﷻ is saying, I have the authority to be proud because I have sovereignty and power over the universe and secondly, I utilise this sovereignty appropriately with wisdom.

A Hadeeth Qudsi recorded in Abū Dāwood and Ibn Mājah states,

اَلْكِبْرِيَاءُ رِدَائِي، وَالْعَظَمَةُ إِزَارِي، فَمَنْ نَازَعَنِي وَاحِدًا مِنْهُمَا، قَذَفْتُهُ فِي النَّارِ

"Highness is my upper cloak (my garment) and honour is my lower garment, so whoever tries to snatch any of the two garments, I will throw him into the Fire." (Abū Dāwood)

Just ponder over this Hadeeth Qudsi for a moment as to how Allāh ﷻ becomes enraged when a person starts to boast. It does not behove a believer to express arrogance at all costs.

An Inspiring Incident

Allāh ﷻ mentions a particular incident in the Holy Qur'ān regarding the Sahābah ﷺ that occurred in the Battle of Hunain. For the first time, the Muslims outnumbered their enemies. The Muslims numbered 12,000 whereas the enemies were only 4,000. Some of the Muslims became over confident that they will surely be victorious in this battle due to their great numbers. So momentarily, their complete reliance upon Allāh ﷻ shifted towards their great numbers. As a result, Allāh's ﷻ help and assistance was removed to test the believers. Allāh ﷻ says,

$$\text{لَقَدْ نَصَرَكُمُ اللهُ فِي مَوَاطِنَ كَثِيرَةٍ وَيَوْمَ حُنَيْنٍ إِذْ أَعْجَبَتْكُمْ كَثْرَتُكُمْ فَلَمْ تُغْنِ عَنكُمْ شَيْئًا}$$

Verily, Allāh assisted you on many occasions and the day of Hunain; when your excessive number astounded you, hence, nothing availed you (due to your increase in number of soldiers). (9:25)

Allāhu Akbar! In this battle the Holy Prophet ﷺ, the leader of mankind, was himself present and the Sahābah ﷺ were in the battlefield but just for a slight moment, when this destructive spiritual disease of pride came into them, Allāh ﷻ tested them, hence, the battle was initially in favour of the enemies. It was only thereafter, when they repented and turned towards Allāh ﷻ, that Allāh ﷻ returned His assistance to them.

From this, we can see the detrimental effects of pride. Thus, there is a great need to eliminate this detrimental spiritual illness of pride. This can be achieved through the guidance and support of a competent Shaykh and spiritual mentor.

Shaykh Muhammad-Ullāh's ﷺ Visit to Shaykh Ashraf Ali Thānwi ﷺ

After graduating from Dārul-Uloom, Deoband, Shaykh Muhammad-Ullāh ﷺ, a great disciple and student of Hakeemul–Ummah, Shaykh Ashraf Ali Thānwi ﷺ embarked on a journey to Thāna Bhawan for his spiritual reformation. He himself relates, "When I entered the Khānqah of Shaykh Thānwi ﷺ, he, after my introduction, said that I had pride in me. I was more than happy to accept the diagnosis of the spiritual ailment and obviously, waited for its remedy. He ordered me to straighten the shoes of the Musallis (worshippers) who attended the Masjid. Moreover, after my Fardh Salāh, in front of the congregation, I had to stand up daily and request the audience to pray for my cure from pride. I continued this for 2 weeks, after which I went and sat in his company. He looked at me and said, 'Half the pride has left; continue the prescription for another two weeks.' I continued for another two weeks, after which, he advised me to work on the other spiritual ailments."

Allāhu Akbar!! This very same person eventually became one of the prominent Walis (friend) of Allāh ﷻ from whom millions of people benefitted, especially the people of Bangladesh.

I was very fortunate to meet him. I can recall the moment when he passed his blessed hand over my head and prayed for my success and for the completion of my Hifz. It was the year 1985 when

Shaykh Muhammad-Ullāh ﷺ came to the UK and was scheduled for a day in Bradford. I could still remember that auspicious day and the meeting of the great Shaykh. Even though I was very young, I could feel the greatness and the Noor of Tawādhu (humility) on his blessed face and in his actions. When he entered the Masjid, there was pin drop silence. All the renowned scholars immediately became silent, leaving the pulpit for the Shaykh.

Putting these two incidents together, i.e. his effort and sacrifice of reformation in the presence of Shaykh Ashraf Ali Thānwi ﷺ and his spiritual elevation in his latter days really left me in admiration.

Shaykh Sayyid Sulaimān Nadwi's ﷺ Visit to Shaykh Ashraf Ali Thānwi ﷺ

Shaykh Sayyid Sulaimān Nadwi ﷺ a great scholar of Islām took the oath of allegiance to Shaykh Ashraf Ali Thānwi ﷺ in the latter part of his life. He asked Shaykh Ashraf Ali Thānwi ﷺ what Tasawwuf was. Shaykh Ashraf Ali Thānwi ﷺ replied, "How can a student like me reply to this question posed by a great scholar of your calibre? Nevertheless, I will merely quote what I heard from my elders. Tasawwuf is to erase oneself. When a person thinks, 'I'm nothing', then he is everything and when a person thinks, 'I'm something', then he is nothing."

For this reason this great scholar, Shaykh Ashraf Ali Thānwi ﷺ says, "I am worse than all Muslims at present and worse than even the disbelievers and animals in terms of the future. In other words, I am worse than all Muslims at present, meaning that it is possible that the person I am despising might possess such a quality which I am not aware of because of which, he is close and beloved to Allāh ﷻ. Secondly, it is possible that Allāh ﷻ gives the Tawfeeq to accept Imān to the disbeliever that I am belittling and then, he reaches a higher status than me."

If we can remember these two amazing sentences of Shaykh Ashraf Ali Thānwi ؒ then, Inshā-Allāh, it will help us considerably in removing this destructive disease of pride from our hearts.

Status of Sayyidunā Abū Zar ؓ

Once Jibreel ؑ came to meet the Holy Prophet ﷺ. During the meeting, Sayyidunā Abū Zar ؓ proceeded towards the Majlis (gathering). Jibreel ؑ said,

$$\text{هٰذَا ابُوْ ذَرٍّ قَدْ اَقْبَلَ}$$

"This is Abū Zar who has approached."

The Holy Prophet ﷺ said (in amazement),

$$\text{اَوَ تَعْرِفُوْنَه}$$

"Do you know him?"

Jibreel ؑ replied,

$$\text{هُوَ اَشْهَرُ عِنْدِنَا مِنْهُ عَنْدَكُمْ}$$

"He is more famous within our circle (of Angels) than he is amongst you."

The Holy Prophet ﷺ asked,

$$بِمَاذَا نَالَ هٰذِهِ الفَضِيْلَةَ$$

"How did he achieve this virtue?"

Jibreel ؑ replied, "(He achieved this due to two reasons:)

$$لِصِغَرِهٖ فِیْ نَفْسِهٖ وَكَثْرَةِ قِرَأَتِهٖ قُلْ هُوَ اللهُ اَحَدٌ$$

"Thinking low of himself and (also) his excessive recitation of Surah Ikhlās."

The Humility of Our Pious Predecessors

Our pious predecessors always considered themselves low. They humbled themselves in front of the Creator and the creation, because of which Allāh ﷻ elevated them.

Junaid Baghdādi ؒ was once in the Masjid. Someone announced that the one who is the worst sinner and most wicked person should come quickly out of the Masjid. Junaid Baghdādi ؒ was the first one out of the Masjid and declared, "I am the worst Muslim." Allāhu Akbar!! In reality, he was amongst the renowned saints of his era from whom multitudes of people benefitted spiritually.

This is in great contrast to today's attitude. Once a person begins to perform his daily Fardh Salāh, perform Hajj and keep a beard according to Sunnah, he starts to belittle others for not doing so. What right have we got? We must constantly remind ourselves of the words of Shaykh Ashraf Ali Thānwi ﷺ, in order to instil Tawādhu (humbleness) in ourselves. We have no idea of what our end result wil become. Mufti Shafee Sāhib ﷺ relates that Imām Fakhr-uddeen Rāzi ﷺ writes: Once, a pious person was dying and the people around him started to carry out the Talqeen (reminding him of the Kalimah), but each time he would reply, "Not yet." When he gained consciousness, they enquired from him as to why he refused to recite the Kalimah. The pious person replied, "I was replying to the Shaytān who attempted to misguide me by saying you have come out of my clutches. Thus, I responded to the Shaytān by saying, 'Not yet' because my Rooh (soul) has not yet been extracted from my body. I still have the fear of Shaytān deviating me and thus, dying a bad death."

The Virtues of Humility
The Holy Prophet ﷺ said,

مَنْ تَوَاضَعَ لِلّٰهِ رَفَعَهُ اللهُ، فَهُوَ فِيْ نَفْسِهٖ صَغِيْرٌ، وَفِيْ أَعْيُنِ النَّاسِ عَظِيْمٌ، وَمَنْ تَكَبَّرَ وَضَعَهُ اللهُ، فَهُوَ فِيْ أَعْيُنِ النَّاسِ صَغِيْرٌ، وَفِيْ نَفْسِهٖ كَبِيْرٌ، حَتّٰى لَهُوَ أَهْوَنُ عَلَيْهِمْ مِنْ كَلْبٍ أَوْ خِنْزِيْرٍ

"The person who humbles for the sake of Allāh, Allāh will raise him. He is low in his own eyes but high in the eyes of the people. The person who expresses arrogance, then Allāh will degrade him, thus he will be despised and looked down upon by the people, even though he is thinking high of himself, to the extent that he will be more degraded and humiliated than a dog and swine."
(Baihaqi, Mishkāt)

Allāh ﷻ elevates the status and position of the one who expresses and shows humbleness only for His sake. He regards himself to be very low and sinful however, on the account of his humility, Allāh ﷻ exalts him and thus, he becomes respectable in the eyes of people. On the other hand, if he shows arrogance and haughtiness through his words and actions, then Allāh ﷻ will disgrace and humiliate him.

The word 'تَكَبَّرَ' comes from the Arabic scale of تَفَعَّل which implies the خَاصِّيَت (speciality) of تَكَلُّف (false pretence). It would thus imply, this person who in reality has no highness or status, is pretending and imagining himself to be someone great. How can we boast about ourselves, when the fact is that we have been created from an impure substance?

An Inspiring Incident

This reminds me of the incident of Yazeed Ibn Muhallab ؓ who says, "I was walking haughtily when I came across a pious friend of Allāh ﷻ, Mutarrif ؓ, who cautioned me. 'Son, do not walk like this, Allāh ﷻ doesn't like this type of attitude and walking haughtily.' I retorted, 'Don't you know who I am?' Mutarrif ؓ replied, 'Without a doubt I know who you are;

اَوَّلُكَ نُطْفَةٌ قَذِرَةٌ. وَاٰخِرُكَ جِيْفَةٌ مَذِرَةٌ، وَاَنْتَ بَيْنَ ذٰلِكَ حَامِلُ عَذِرَةٍ

'Your beginning is an impure semen, your ending is a decomposed corpse and in between, you are carrying waste in your body.'"

Allāhu Akbar! What a beautiful answer he gave! This is worth engraving in gold and keeping with us all the time to constantly remind ourselves about our reality. This will surely eradicate the destructive malady of pride from our hearts.

This is exactly what Allāh ﷻ reminds us of in the Holy Qur'ān when He reprimands mankind for being so ungrateful. He says ;

$$\text{قُتِلَ الْإِنْسَانُ مَا أَكْفَرَهُ مِنْ أَيِّ شَيْءٍ خَلَقَهُ مِنْ نُطْفَةٍ خَلَقَهُ فَقَدَّرَهُ}$$

May man be destroyed; how ungrateful he is! From which substance has he been created? From an impure semen, Allāh has created him and then fashioned him (proportionately). (80:17-19)

Thus, it is clear how detrimental and serious pride is, to the extent that it makes a person become worse than dogs and pigs in the sight of Allāh ﷻ and above all, he will not be able to enter Paradise.

What is Takabbur (Pride)?

In a Hadeeth of Muslim, the Holy Prophet ﷺ says,

$$\text{لَا يَدْخُلُ الْجَنَّةَ مَنْ كَانَ فِي قَلْبِهِ مِثْقَالُ ذَرَّةٍ مِنْ كِبْرٍ قَالَ رَجُلٌ: إِنَّ الرَّجُلَ يُحِبُّ أَنْ يَكُونَ ثَوْبُهُ حَسَنًا وَنَعْلُهُ حَسَنَةً. قَالَ: إِنَّ اللهَ جَمِيلٌ يُحِبُّ الْجَمَالَ، الْكِبْرُ بَطَرُ الْحَقِّ وَغَمْطُ النَّاسِ}$$

"A person will not enter Paradise who has a mustard seed amount of pride in his heart." A person asked, "O' Rasūlullāh ﷺ, (what if) a person desires his clothes to be good and his shoes to be good (is this classed as pride)?" The Holy Prophet ﷺ replied, "Indeed, Allāh is beautiful and He loves beauty. In reality, pride is to reject the truth and belittle people." (Muslim)

Takabbur (pride) is like an atom bomb which destroys all our actions. If it is known that in your house there is an atom bomb, then what will you do? You will immediately call for the bomb disposal squad to remove the dangerous item from your house. The rest of your valuables will be of no use if the atom bomb is present. Similarly, pride will destroy all our actions which we have carried out. So what is the solution and how can we eliminate it? We will need the spiritual bomb disposal squad (these are the Mashāikh - the scholars of Tasawwuf) to get rid of this atomic bomb from our hearts, in order for us to preserve all the rest of our deeds and to keep them intact and safe.

Qualities of a Spiritual Shaykh

What are the qualities of the pious friends of Allāh ﷻ? Allāh ﷻ says,

وَعِبَادُ الرَّحْمٰنِ الَّذِيْنَ يَمْشُوْنَ عَلَى الْأَرْضِ هَوْنًا

The true servants of the Most Merciful are those who walk on the earth with humility. (25:63)

They do not stroll upon the earth with haughtiness and arrogance, as Allāh ﷻ says;

وَلَا تَمْشِ فِي الْأَرْضِ مَرَحًا إِنَّكَ لَنْ تَخْرِقَ الْأَرْضَ وَلَنْ تَبْلُغَ الْجِبَالَ طُوْلًا

> Do not walk haughtily on the surface of the earth; you will not be able to cleave the ground nor will you be able to reach the mountains in height. (17:37)

When the Holy Prophet ﷺ explained that a proud person will not be able to enter Paradise, a person enquired, "What if a person likes to keep his clothes in a good condition and wants to have good quality shoes (then will this be classified as pride)?" The Holy Prophet ﷺ replied, "No, because Allāh ﷻ is Beautiful and He loves beauty," in other words, He loves cleanliness. A person must maintain cleanliness at all times and there is no problem with wearing nice clothes.

What is pride? The Holy Prophet ﷺ defined the meaning of pride and encapsulated it in two important elements:

1) بَطَرُ الْحَقِّ (Rejecting the truth)

When one is informed regarding a Mas'alah or injunction of Allāh ﷻ which is correct, then he rejects it. There are many people who we see and hear that say, "I will never accept this ruling even if all the Muftis and scholars explain it to me." How stubborn and ignorant can a person become? Allāh ﷻ save us from this calamity.

2) غَمْطُ النَّاسِ (Belittling people)

It is common amongst us that we tend to praise a person in his presence but immediately after leaving the Majlis (gathering), we hurl all kinds of allegations against him and ridicule and mock at him. This is a very grave sin. Just imagine for a moment that if a person honours you, whilst at the same time expresses ill feelings towards your children, by rebuking and uttering offensive remarks to them, would you ever bring such an individual close to you? Would you ever show your love and affection towards him? Definitely not! Likewise, Allāh ﷻ does not love that person who engages in such an evil habit.

The Hadeeth says;

الْخَلْقُ عِيَالُ اللهِ، فَأَحَبُّ الْخَلْقِ إِلَى اللهِ مَنْ أَحْسَنَ إِلَى عِيَالِه

"The entire creation is the family of Allāh. The most beloved to Allāh is the one who is loving and caring to His family members." (Shua'bul Imān)

So therefore, if someone belittles any person, then he is despising the creation of Allāh ﷻ – which Allāh ﷻ dislikes and hates.

The Holy Prophet ﷺ stated 'وَغَمْطُ النَّاسِ' (belittling the people) and not 'وَغَمْطُ الْمُسْلِمِ' (belittling the Muslim) which includes even non-Muslims. It is not permissible even to belittle non-Muslims. We should dislike the act of Kufr (disbelief) but not the Kāfir (disbelievers) and similarly, we should hate the act of Fisq (transgression) but not the Fāsiq (transgressor). Hence, to reprimand upon a sin or evil is Wājib (compulsory) but at the same time to belittle the person is Harām (forbidden).

A Question Posed to Shaykh Ashraf Ali Thānwi ❦

A person questioned Shaykh Ashraf Ali Thānwi ❦ that how is it possible for us to dislike a person perpetrating the sin but at the same time, not dislike the sinner. The Shaykh replied, "There is nothing complex and intricate about this. Take the example of a handsome young prince who has ink on his face. You will dislike the ink but not the prince himself and will suggest to him to remove the ink from his face with soap. Immediately thereafter, he will become the same handsome prince he once was. If the moon becomes concealed by the cloud, does anyone belittle it? Likewise, with a sinful person, he might indulge in sins and evil acts but if he repents sincerely and sheds a few tears, he will immediately reach the status of the pious servants. We have no right to belittle any of Allāh's ﷻ creation."

No slave has the right or the authority to put a price on himself because this is the sole right of Allāh ﷻ. Only Allāh ﷻ knows the status of each person. When Allāh ﷻ declares anyone to be His true servant, only then will it be recognised and accepted.

A Girl Getting Married

Shāh Abdul Ghani ❦, an eminent Khaleefah (disciple) of Shaykh Thānwi ❦, says that there was a girl who was getting married. All the female members from her locality came to beautify her and dress her. After applying all the makeup and dressing, they started to applaud her and praise her for her exceptional beauty by remarking, "You are absolutely gorgeous," etc. The girl, now a bride, started to cry. Her friends asked her the reason for her crying. She replied, "You praising me doesn't make me happy because true happiness and joy will be when my husband glances at me and he expresses his happiness. Only then will I become the happiest woman in the world."

After narrating this incident, Shaykh Abdul Ghani Sāhib ؒ started to weep and remarked, "If all the world praises me, respects me and honours me but my Allāh ﷻ is displeased with me, then what have I gained? I have lost everything. Only when Allāh ﷻ, in the Hereafter says, "Congratulations My servant; you have become successful, then that is the true success. He says,

$$\text{فَمَنْ زُحْزِحَ عَنِ النَّارِ وَأُدْخِلَ الْجَنَّةَ فَقَدْ فَازَ}$$

Whoever is saved from the Hellfire and entered into Paradise shall truly be successful. (3:185)

A person should never boast after worshipping Allāh ﷻ or after performing good deeds. It must be remembered that if pride creeps into the heart, after performing a good deed, this will be a sign of that action being disapproved by Allāh ﷻ.

The Famous Du'ā of Sayyidunā Ibrāheem ؑ

We have an excellent example of the sincerity and humbleness of Sayyidunā Ibrāheem ؑ and Sayyidunā Ismāeel ؑ, when they constructed the House of Allāh ﷻ - one of the greatest deeds on the surface of the earth. Upon its completion, they supplicated to Allāh

🌺 for its acceptance in the following manner;

$$\text{رَبَّنَا تَقَبَّلْ مِنَّا إِنَّكَ أَنتَ السَّمِيعُ الْعَلِيمُ}$$

O' our Lord, accept (this deed) from us. Indeed, You are the All-Hearing and All-Knowing. (2:122)

Allāmah Āloosi 🌺 comments in his Tafseer, Roohul Ma'āni, that the usage of the word, 'Taqabbal' (O' Allāh 🌺 accept) comes from the Bāb (scale) of Tafa'ul. Here, it denotes to confession of ones inability and shortcoming. So, Ibrāheem 🌺 and Ismāeel 🌺 prayed, "O' Allah 🌺, though this deed is not worthy of being accepted, out of Your Infinite Mercy, please accept it. We have no rights or authority to demand from You but through Your benevolence, accept this small deed of ours.

$$\text{إِنَّكَ أَنتَ السَّمِيعُ الْعَلِيمُ}$$

You are the All-Hearing and All-Knowing.

In other words,

$$\text{سَمِيعٌ بِدَعْوَاتِنَا، عَلِيمٌ بِنِيَّاتِنَا}$$

"You are the One Who listens to our prayers and supplications and You are the One Who knows our intentions (for what reason we have carried out this deed)."

We must not harbour any form of pride in our hearts after performing a good deed. Rather, we should beseech Allāh 🌺 with the same Du'ā as the two beloved Messengers did. Inshā-Allāh 🌺, the seed of pride will eventually disappear from our hearts.

The Nature of Ujb (Vanity)

At this point, it is necessary to mention some remedies for this spiritual ailment and also, to relate an eye-opening incident of what it truly means not to harbour pride or Ujb (vanity). However, first of all, what is Ujb (vanity)? Ujb is the attribution of excellence to oneself whilst being oblivious of the possibility that such excellence can be snatched away by Allāh ﷻ. Ujb is a cloaked and subtle trick of the human ego, with the aspiration to occupy a distinguishing rank above others (or in the eyes of others).

Ujb resembles pride in all aspects, except that Ujb does not necessarily imply that others are inferior (as opposed to Takabbur). A person harbouring Ujb considers himself to be of a lofty rank without necessarily regarding others to be inferior.

Shaykh Shihāb-Uddeen Suhorwardi ﷺ gave two advices to his disciples:
1) Never become self-conceited.
2) Never look down upon anyone else.

Shaykh Ashraf Ali Thānwi ﷺ says, "It is not right for any person to be proud of his position and achievements and despise others. Our Imān is not of our own earning, rather, it is merely Allāh's ﷻ Infinite Grace endowed to us and Allāh ﷻ can remove it from us whenever He wishes."

An Incident of Deep Reflection

The following incident is enriched with lessons and warnings, especially for those in high positions of academic activities, traversing the spiritual path or undertaking any other Deeni services. These people, particularly should truly derive benefit and guidance from this and realise the harmful effects of despising others.

It was at the end of the second century Hijri, not too long after the era of the Holy Prophet ﷺ and the Sahābahs ؓ, when there was an era flourished with people of piety, trust and righteousness, including the great four Imāms of Islām, Fuqahā (Jurists) and Muhaddithoon (Hadeeth scholars). In every town, there were numerous Ulamā and pious men, especially in cities such as Baghdad, which was at that time, the capital city of Islamic learning. This city, with all its internal and external virtues, was truly a jewel of the world. Baghdād was indeed a central headquarter for the righteous ones and a gathering place for the Jurists, Hadeeth scholars and the saintly ones.

On the one hand, ones eyes were delighted with the views of beautiful buildings, whilst on the other hand, one would enjoy the pleasures of being in the gatherings of the scholars and pious men in their study circles of learning and Madāris (Islamic institute) and the sounds of Dhikr and Tilāwat.

In this city, there was a prominent figure by the name Abū Abdullāh Andalusi ؒ - a renowned spiritual mentor of almost all the people of Iraq. He was also a great scholar and a Muhaddith. It is mentioned that his students and Mureeds (disciples) reached up to approximately twelve thousand. Apart from the fact that he was a man of great piety, he was also a renowned scholar. He had memorised over thirty thousand Ahādeeth and also, recited the Holy Qur'ān in all the various forms of Qirā'at.

On one occasion, he was travelling on a journey and was accompanied by a large crowd of students and Mureeds, among whom was Junaid Baghdādi ❀ and Shibli ❀. Shibli ❀ relates: "Our caravan was travelling comfortably until we passed by an area where Christians were resting. It was already time for Salāh, but because of the unavailability of water, we were unable to perform it yet. Upon reaching the village of the Christians, we began the search for water. We went about the village and later, discovered the town had many temples and churches in which sun worshippers, Jews, cross-worshipping Christians and their religious leaders were gathered. Some of them worshipped the sun, some were worshipping fire and some of them were directing their pleas towards the cross. When we saw all this, we were greatly surprised at the lack of understanding and reason of these people.

However, we continued until we reached to the outskirts of the town, where we found a well with a few girls drawing water for people to drink. Shaykh Abū Abdullāh saw one of the girls who stood out from the rest, through her exquisite beauty. She was well dressed in beautiful clothes and decorated with jewels. The Shaykh asked the other girls who she was. They replied, 'This is the daughter of our Chief.' The Shaykh replied, 'Then why did her father degrade her to such an extent that she has to sit at a well and give people water to drink? Does he not have a maid or servant who can do this?' The girls said, 'Yes, he has servants but her father is a very intelligent person. He does not want her to sit down and be proud and boastful over her father's possessions and thus, corrupt her character. He does not want that after marriage, she should fail in her duty of looking after her husband's goods.'"

Shibli ؓ says, "The Shaykh sat down with his head bent forward and remained silent like that for three days without eating, drinking or talking to anyone. At Salāh time, he performed his Salāh. On the third day, becoming despondent of his situation, I decided to speak to him. I said, 'O' Shaykh, your disciples and students are very worried and perplexed of you continuous silence. Please speak to us as to what is the problem?'

The Shaykh replied, 'My dear friends! For how long can I keep my condition hidden from you? My heart has become filled with love for the girl we saw the day before yesterday. So much has this love filled my whole being that it is in control of all my limbs. It is not possible for me under any circumstances to depart from here.'

I replied, 'O' our leader! You are the spiritual guide of all of Iraq. You are known all over for your piety, knowledge and virtues. Your disciples are over twelve thousand. I beg of you, through the Holy Qur'ān, do not disgrace us.'

The Shaykh said, 'My dear friends, your portion and my portion has already been sealed by fate. The cloak of sainthood has been removed from me and the signs of Hidāyat (guidance) have been taken away from me. What has been predestined has come to pass. Now I am nothing.' Saying this, the Shaykh began weeping bitterly. We were thoroughly shocked at this and in sorrow, we all started crying and the Shaykh cried with us, so much that the very earth beneath our feet became wet with our tears. We were forced to return home.

When the people heard of our return, they appeared in large numbers at the outskirts of the city to meet the Shaykh. They saw that he was not amongst us and enquired about it. We informed them of the incident that occurred. Upon informing them, there was loud wailing and crying. So great was the sorrow that many of his Mureeds (disciples) died instantly. The others fell down in prayers and Du'ā, begging Allāh ﷻ to guide the Shaykh and return him to his former position.

In the meantime, all the Khānqhas closed down. We were all still talking about the Shaykh's tragedy and a year later, some of us decided to go and find out how and where the Shaykh was. A group of us set forth and we went to the village where we had left him. We asked the people and they told us that he was in the woods looking after pigs.

We said, 'Allāh ﷻ protect us! What is this that has happened?' The villagers replied, 'He proposed marriage to the daughter of the chief of the village. The girl's father accepted the proposal on condition that he looks after the pigs.'

We heard this and were shocked, with tears streaming from our eyes. Taking courage and inspite of our sorrow, we went to the woods where he was rearing pigs. We saw him with a hat of the

Christians around his neck. He stood leaning on a staff as he watched the pigs, standing in the manner in which he stood when he used to deliver the Khutbah for us. This was like rubbing salt into our open wounds.

When he saw us coming towards him, he bent his head in shame. We came nearer and said to him, 'Assalāmu Alaikum.' He replied in a soft voice, 'Wa alaikumus Salām.'

I said, 'O' Shaykh! Inspite of all your knowledge, virtue, Hadeeth and Tafseer, what is this that has happened to you?'

He replied, 'My dear brothers! Now, I am not driven by my own choice and will. Whatever Allāh ﷻ has destined for me has come to pass. After drawing me close to His door, He has now thrown me far away from Him. Who is there that can turn the decree of Allāh ﷻ? O' my brothers! Fear Allāh's ﷻ Great Power and Wrath. Never become proud and arrogant over your knowledge and virtue.' Then turning towards the Heavens, he said, 'O' my Lord! I never expected that You will make me so disgraceful and despised and cast me away from Your door.' The Shaykh began crying bitterly and appealing to Allāh ﷻ. He then remarked, 'O' Shibli! Observe others and take warnings (in the Hadeeth we are told: Blessed is that person who takes a lesson from the condition of others).

Due to crying, I could barely speak and replied, 'O' Lord, we seek help from You and from You do we beseech. In everything we depend upon You. Remove this tragedy from us as there is none who can dispel it except You!'

When the pigs heard all this crying they gathered around us and started jumping around, all the while, oinking so loud that the whole forest began echoing with their sounds.

I asked the Shaykh, 'Shaykh, you used to recite the Qur'ān in seven different Qirāts. Do you still have any verses in your mind?'

He replied, 'I do not remember anything else of the Holy Qur'ān except two verses,

$$وَمَنْ يُهِنِ اللّٰهُ فَمَا لَهُ مِنْ مُكْرِمٍ إِنَّ اللّٰهَ يَفْعَلُ مَا يَشَاءُ$$

Whosoever Allāh disgraces, no one can grant him honour. Indeed Allāh does as He pleases. (22:18)

$$وَمَنْ يَتَبَدَّلِ الْكُفْرَ بِالْإِيمَانِ فَقَدْ ضَلَّ سَوَاءَ السَّبِيلِ$$

The one who exchanges Imān for Kufr (disbelief) has certainly strayed from the straight path. (2:108)

I further asked, 'O' Shaykh, you used to remember thirty thousand Ahādeeth with their Sanads (chain of narrators) by heart. Do you still remember them?'

He replied, "Only one.

Seeing the Shaykh in that condition, myself and the others departed for Baghdād in despair and sorrow. We were on route back, after having travelled across about three manzils (48 miles), when all of a sudden, we saw the Shaykh in front of us emerging from a river, where he had just performed Ghusl. In a loud voice he said, 'I bear witness that there is none worthy of worship besides Allāh and I bear witness that Muhammad ﷺ is the Messenger of Allāh ﷻ.'

Only those individuals who had seen our hopelessness, sorrow and heartache would truly appreciate what happiness this sight brought us. We became overjoyed. The Shaykh came closer to us and said, 'Give me a piece of clean clothing to wear.'

The Shaykh put on the clean clothes and started performing Salāh, while we impatiently waited to hear his story. It was only after he performed Salāh that we heard the story. He turned to us and we said, 'All praises be to Allāh ﷻ Who returned you to us and re-united us once again, after our Jamā'at (group) broke off. Inform us, how is it that inspite of our pleads to you to come back, you refused very strongly and now you have returned?'

The Shaykh replied, 'My friends, when you people left me, I fell down and in tears I begged Allāh ﷻ to save me from that tragedy. I begged: "Lord, I am Your sinful slave.' Allāh ﷻ, Who is the Hearer of all Du'ās, finally accepted my plea and wiped out my faults.'
We said, 'Please tell us the reason for this trial?'

The Shaykh replied, 'When we arrived to that village and saw the temples, synagogues, churches and the fire worshippers and cross worshippers engaged in worshiping things besides Allāh ﷻ, an element of pride overtook my heart in that we are the worshippers of

One Allāh ﷻ. I thought for a moment that these foolish people are wretched, doomed and ignorant fools to worship lifeless and brainless beings. At that time, I heard a voice inside me telling me, 'This Imān which you have is not part of your virtue or good qualities. All these are merely Our favours upon you, so do not consider your faith to be of your own earning, so that you may look down upon them with despising eyes. If you wish, We can test you!' At that moment, I felt as if an object had left my heart and flew away. That was in fact my Imān.'

Thereafter, our caravan arrived in Baghdad with great joy all around us. All of the Mureeds became extremely happy that the Shaykh had once again, re-embraced Islām. The Khānqahs were again opened. The king of the time came and visited the Shaykh and brought some presents. The Shaykh resumed his previous activities such as the tutoring of the Holy Qur'ān and Hadeeth and he occupied himself with rectification services. Allāh ﷻ returned to him his previous treasure of knowledge and in addition, more wisdom and greater depth in his knowledge. Within a short period, the number of his students exceeded to forty thousand."

Shaykh Ashraf Ali Thānwi ﷺ, after recording this incident says, "When this is the situation (of such high ranking ones), then can one claim that the present situation which we are in, is of our own independent choice?" Verily, everything is in the control of Allāh ﷻ and He grants honour to whosoever He wishes.

Cure for Pride

Before concluding, I would like to mention some prescriptions prescribed by our pious predecessors to eradicate this dangerous spiritual ailment. To do this, we need to first contemplate and ponder over the following major points. Always remember that pride is developed due to a quality or virtue one possesses on the account of which one thinks great of oneself whilst belittling others. These following points should be considered and contemplated upon:

1) I have this certain quality which others do not have but I have not gained this through my efforts. It was Divinely bestowed.

2) I am not worthy of this great blessing rather, it has been endowed to me through Allāh's ﷻ Infinite Mercy.

3) After attaining this particular virtue and quality, it is not permanent nor in my control. Allāh ﷻ can take this away from me whenever He wishes.

4) Even though the person whom I belittle does not have this virtue at present, it is very possible that in the near future, he is endowed with this virtue and surpasses my status.

5) Or, even at present, he may surpass me in status on the account of other qualities which he has that are hidden from me.

6) If no excellence of this person comes to mind, then it is very possible that he is Maqbool (accepted) by Allāh ﷻ whilst I am not. So I

have no reason to belittle him.

7) If by chance, this particular person or group whom I belittle, or think low of in every aspect are in fact, lower than me, then this should make me more affectionate towards them. This is because an accomplished and professional person has the responsibility to express his affection and love towards those who are lower than him. Once love becomes binding, then hopefully there will be no hatred or belittling one another.

8) If the above prescriptions cannot be followed, then occasionally go and meet the person with a cheerful countenance. Have a healthy dialogue with him and after bonding the relationship, love will eventually replace hatred and the notion of belittlement towards him will eventually fade away.

May Allāh ﷻ give us the Tawfeeq (ability) to remove this spiritual ailment and may Allāh ﷻ instil Tawādhu (humbleness) and sincerity in the place of pride. Āmeen!

Cure for Anger

وَالْكَاظِمِيْنَ الْغَيْظَ وَالْعَافِيْنَ عَنِ النَّاسِ وَاللّٰهُ يُحِبُّ الْمُحْسِنِيْنَ

"And those who subdue their anger and pardon people and Allāh loves those who do Ihsān (righteous deeds)." (3:134)

Introduction

Allāh ﷻ states in the Holy Qur'ān;

$$\text{وَالْكَاظِمِينَ الْغَيْظَ وَالْعَافِينَ عَنِ النَّاسِ وَاللهُ يُحِبُّ الْمُحْسِنِينَ}$$

And those who subdue their anger and pardon people and Allāh loves those who do Ihsān (righteous deeds). (3:134)

In this verse, Allāh ﷻ points out three special qualities of His chosen servants:

1) They subdue their anger.
2) They forgive the mistakes of other servants.
3) They not only forgive them, but also show kindness and generosity towards them.

These are the people who Allāh ﷻ loves. In the above verse, Allāh ﷻ has outlined a cure for the detrimental spiritual illness of anger. He says وَالْكَاظِمِينَ الْغَيْظَ those who subdue the anger.

What is the meaning of وَالْكَاظِمِينَ الْغَيْظَ? According to the rules of Arabic Grammar, when Alif Lām appears on an Ism Fā'il, it conveys the meaning of Ism Mawsool, hence the meaning would be,

$$\text{اَلَّذِينَ يَكْظِمُونَ الْغَيْظَ}$$

Those who suppress the anger.

It is important to understand that becoming angry is not bad. Rather, channelling and utilizing it in the wrong place is bad and blameworthy. If anger was something despised, then instead of revealing وَالْكَاظِمِيْنَ الْغَيْظَ, وَالْعَادِمِيْنَ الْغَيْظَ would have been revealed, meaning those who completely eradicate their anger from the roots. The Scholars of Tafseer say that the objective is not to eliminate anger completely, but to use in its appropriate places.

Now, what does the Arabic word وَالْكَاظِمِيْنَ mean? Allāmah Āloosi ؒ writes in his Tafseer, Roohul Ma'āni, that the root word كَظَمَ is used in the Arabic language when a water vessel or bottle is full to the top and begins to spill out. The Arabs would tie the top of the water bottle with a rope or string to avoid any spillage. The word كَظَمَ means;

شَدُّ رَأْسِ الْقِرْبَةِ عِنْدَ امْتِلَائِهَا

"To fasten and tie the top of the water bottle when it is completely full."

Thus Allāh ﷻ is saying, "When you become angry and your water vessel (i.e. body) starts to utter foul language in anger, then tie your mouth with the rope of 'Kazm' (by using silence) and suppress and restrain your anger."

Reward for Restraining Anger

The Holy Prophet ﷺ said;

$$\text{مَنْ كَظَمَ غَيْظًا وَهُوَ يَقْدِرُ عَلَى إِنْفَاذِهِ مَلَأَهُ اللهُ تَعَالَى قَلْبَهُ أَمْنًا وَإِيمَانًا}$$

"The person who suppresses his anger whilst he has the power to execute it, Allāh ﷻ will fill his heart with tranquillity and Imān."
(Jāmi Sagheer)

Anger which is for the sake of Allāh ﷻ and His Deen is exempted from this. Hence, the Holy Prophet ﷺ would become angry when the disobedience of Allāh ﷻ occured as described in a Hadeeth,

$$\text{كَأَنَّ الرُّمَّانَ عُصِرَ عَلَى وَجْهِهِ}$$

"As though pomegranate seeds were sprinkled over his blessed face."

In another Hadeeth, the Holy Prophet ﷺ said,

$$\text{إِنَّ الْغَضَبَ لَيُفْسِدُ الْإِيمَانَ كَمَا يُفْسِدُ الصَّبْرُ الْعَسَلَ}$$

"Indeed anger destroys Imān the same way that the aloe plant destroys honey." (Baihaqi)

The aloe plant has a very bitter taste. If a drop of aloe plant is mixed with a kilo of honey, then all the honey will become bitter. Likewise, anger transforms the sweetness of Imān to a bitter poison and ultimately, takes away the sweetness and joy of recitation of the Holy Qur'ān, worshipping Allāh ﷻ and all that which is connected to Imān. Sometimes, it could actually lead to the destruction of ones faith.

Cure for Anger — Disciplining Ones Servant

In a Hadeeth recorded in Mishkāt, it mentions the glad tidings of the punishment being averted from a person who restrains his anger. How tremendous is this reward! The Holy Prophet ﷺ says,

$$\text{مَنْ كَفَّ غَضَبَهُ كَفَّ اللهُ عَنْهُ عَذَابَهُ يَوْمَ الْقِيَامَةِ}$$

Whosoever restrains his anger, Allāh ﷻ will restrain his punishment from him on the Day of Judgement. (Mishkāt)

Sayyidunā Abū Mas'ood ؓ Disciplining his Slave

Imām Muslim ؓ records an incident narrated by Sayyidunā Abū Mas'ood ؓ who says,

$$\text{كُنْتُ أَضْرِبُ غُلَامًا لِي}$$

"I was hitting one of my slaves with a whip,"

$$\text{فَسَمِعْتُ صَوْتًا مِّنْ خَلْفِي}$$

"When I suddenly heard a voice from behind."

$$\text{اِعْلَمْ، أَبَا مَسْعُودٍ، اَللهُ أَقْدَرُ عَلَيْكَ مِنْكَ عَلَيْهِ}$$

"Understand well, O' Abū Mas'ood. Indeed Allāh has more power and might over you than you have over your slave."

$$\text{فَالْتَفَتُّ فَإِذَا هُوَ رَسُولُ اللهِ صَلَّى اللهُ عَلَيْهِ وَسَلَّمَ}$$

"I immediately turned my back and suddenly it was the Messenger of Allāh."

Sayyidunā Abū Mas'ood ؓ immediately realised his shortcoming and as an atonement for his mistake, he declared,

$$يَا رَسُوْلَ اللهِ، هُوَ حُرٌّ لِوَجْهِ اللهِ$$

"O Messenger of Allāh! He is free for the sake of Allāh."

The Holy Prophet ﷺ replied,

$$أَمَا لَوْ لَمْ تَفْعَلْ لَلَفَحَتْكَ النَّارُ، أَوْ لَمَسَّتْكَ النَّارُ$$

"If you did not do this [i.e. free your slave and show your mercy on him], then the fire [of Jahannam] would have [completely] burned you or [he said] the fire would have surely touched you." (Muslim)

Just reflect for a moment who this person was! He was an eminent Companion of the Holy Prophet ﷺ and what did the Holy Prophet ﷺ warn him of? "If you did not show any mercy (upon this slave) then the fire of Jahannam would not spare you." If this is the case with the Prophet's ﷺ Companion, then who from amongst us can say that anger is not detrimental to us spirituality or even mentally?

My dear friends! Nowadays people claim that there is no need for a spiritual guide. Reflect! Did not this prominent Companion, Sayyidunā Abū Mas'ood ؓ require a guide, even though the Companions were the best people after the Prophets?

Sayyidunā Abū Bakr ؓ Restrains His Anger

Sayyidunā Abū Bakr ؓ once became angry with his relative, Mistah ؓ, who was also unfortunately, amongst those who were involved in the false accusation of Sayyidah Āishah ؓ. After Allāh ﷻ declared her innocence in the Holy Qur'ān. Sayyidunā Abū Bakr ؓ took a firm oath that he will not spend on him. However, Sayyidunā Mistah ؓ was a participant of Badr whom Allāh ﷻ honoured with a lofty status. Hence Allāh ﷻ interceded on his behalf with the words,

$$\text{اَلَا تُحِبُّوْنَ اَنْ يَّغْفِرَ اللّٰهُ لَكُمْ}$$

Would you not love that Allāh forgives you? (24:21)

The Scholars of Tafseer, such as Ibn Katheer ؒ, state that this verse was revealed regarding Sayyidunā Abū Bakr ؓ. In short Allāh ﷻ said, "O' Abū Bakr, do you not like to forgive the mistake of my servant who is a participant of Badr and I, in exchange, forgive your mistakes on the Day of Judgement." When this verse was revealed, Sayyidunā Abū Bakr ؓ broke his promise, paid his Kaffārah and made another oath exclaiming,

$$\text{بَلٰى، وَاللّٰهِ اِنِّيْ اُحِبُّ اَنْ يَّغْفِرَ اللّٰهُ لِيْ}$$

"Why not? By Allāh, I love that Allāh, forgives me."

Therefore, he forgave his cousin-brother, Mistah and from then on, he spent even more on him. This is what Allāh ﷻ means when He says,

Cure for Anger — Zainul Ābideen

وَالْعَافِيْنَ عَنِ النَّاسِ وَاللّٰهُ يُحِبُّ الْمُحْسِنِيْنَ

Those who pardon people and Allāh loves those who do Ihsān (righteous deeds). (3:134)

After forgiving the people, show kindness and generosity the way Siddique Akbar ؓ showed towards his cousin.

Zainul Ābideen ؓ Restrains His Anger

Zainul Ābideen ؓ, the grandson of Sayyidunā Ali ؓ, was performing Wudhu whilst his Khādim (servant) was pouring water for his ablution. It so happened that accidently, the water vessel fell from the Khādim's hands and injured Zainul Ābideen's ؓ head. He looked towards the khādim in anger. Māshā-Allāh, the khādim was a Hāfidh. He immediately recited the verse, وَالْكَاظِمِيْنَ الْغَيْظَ (they suppress their anger). So, Zainul Ābideen ؓ instantly said, قَدْ كَظَمْتُ غَيْظِي (I have restrained my anger). He immediately accepted the command of Allāh ﷻ. He did not for a moment think that he is my khādim; who gives him the authority to order me. Today, the main problem is, we do not want to accept authority or the order of anyone. Rather, it has to come from someone above to accept it. Whoever instructs us, we need to see what the order is and whose order it is. Here, it was the order of Allāh ﷻ even though it came from the mouth of a junior. Hence, Zainul Ābideen ؓ promptly accepted.

The Khādim then recited, وَالْعَافِيْنَ عَنِ النَّاسِ (and those who pardon people). Zainul Ābideen ؓ replied قَدْ عَفَوْتُ عَنْكَ (I have forgiven your mistake). The khādim concluded by saying وَاللّٰهُ يُحِبُّ الْمُحْسِنِيْنَ (Allāh ﷻ loves the ones who do good deeds). Zainul Ābideen ؓ replied اِنَّكَ حُرٌّ لِوَجْهِ اللّٰهِ (You are free for the sake of Allāh ﷻ).

Incidents of the Pious who Restrained their Anger

1: Shaykh Abdul Ghani Phulpoori ؒ, an eminent disciple of Hakeemul-Ummah, Shaykh Ashraf Ali Thānwi ؒ, once became angry with an individual and in anger, he slightly transgressed the limits. Instantly, he realised his mistake and thereafter advanced towards his village to seek forgiveness from the person.

This individual was an ordinary farmer who lived a couple of miles away from the Shaykh's village. However, due to the Shaykh's restlessness, he even forgot the way. He eventually reached the destination and pleaded for forgiveness from him. The farmer was amazed and said, "You are a great scholar and I am just an ordinary, sinful farmer. You are like a father figure to me who has the right to reprimand his son." The Shaykh replied, "Tomorrow (on the Day of Judgement) it will be truly known who is greater. I will not leave until you don't say that you have forgiven me." The man realised that the Shaykh would not leave until he accepted his apology so he said, "It is your order and to make you happy, I say I have forgiven you, even though you have the full right to reprimand me." Only then did the Shaykh return home.

That night, the Shaykh related, "I dreamt of seeing the Holy Prophet ﷺ and Sayyiduna Ali ؓ on one boat and I was alone in another boat at a distance. The Holy Prophet ﷺ called out loudly to

Sayyidunā Ali ﷺ, 'O' Ali, join my boat to Abdul Ghani's boat? When Sayyidunā Ali ﷺ joined the two boats together, the sound of the two boats touching each other echoed in my ears. To this day, I still feel the satisfaction and contentment of the sound of the two boats joining together."

Let us just ponder and imagine the great reward he achieved for his atonement of anger and asking for forgiveness from that farmer.

2: Hakeemul-Ummah Shaykh Ashraf Ali Thānwi ﷺ related in one of his lectures about a man whose wife added too much salt in the food. Rather than unleashing his anger upon her, he forgave her instead for the pleasure of Allāh ﷻ. He did not utter a word of contempt. The Shaykh says that after his death a pious person saw him in his dream and asked, "How did you fare in front of Allāh ﷻ?" He replied, "The situation was drastic and disastrous and all my major sins were exposed. When everything was going negative, Allāh ﷻ said, 'On a particular day, my female servant added too much salt in your food and you forgave her. So today in exchange of that patience and suppressing of your anger, I have forgiven all your sins.'" Subhān-Allāh!

3: Shāh Abul-Hasan Kirqāni ﷺ used to mount on a lion and go into the jungle to fetch fire wood. If the lion showed any negligence in this matter, he used to discipline it with a live snake as a whip.

Once, a person came all the way from Khurrāsān to visit him. Shāh Abul-Hasan's ﷺ wife, who was very bad tempered, asked the man the reason for his visit. He replied that he had come to give Bai'ah (oath of allegiance) to the Shaykh. The wife replied, لاَحَوْلَ وَلاَ قُوَّةَ إِلاَّ بِاللهِ, who in the world knows him better than me? I stay with him day and night. He is a fraudster! Have you got any sense or intelligence? She continued mentioning so many negative things about the Shaykh, making the Mureed cry.

He sobbed and said, "My journey of a thousand miles has gone to waste."

The people of the locality rushed towards him, calmed him down and informed him that the Shaykh's wife was a bad tempered woman and that he should not have any evil thoughts about the Shaykh. They told him to go to the jungle where he will find the Shaykh bringing fire wood. When he reached there, he found the Shaykh mounted on a lion and returning back home.

The Shaykh had Kashf (inspiration of the situation) and asked, "You seemed to be very distraught; what happened?" The Mureed replied, "You have a very bad tempered wife. Why have you married a woman like that?" The Shaykh replied, "The lion I have as a mount and the snake as a whip are the reward of being patient upon the pain of this woman."

4: Shaykh Mazhar Jāne Jā ؒ was a very sensitive person. When the enemy shot a bullet towards him, he was asked, "How did you feel?" He replied, "I didn't feel any pain due to the bullet but the smell of the gunpowder troubled me."

Cure for Anger   Incidents of the Pious

The Rājah (king) of Delhi once came to visit him and after drinking a glass of water, the Rājah put the glass sideways. The Shaykh started to get a headache. The Rājah asked, "Shaykh! I want to present you with a khādim (servant) for your assistance." The Shaykh replied, "I was quiet until now, but I must inform you that when you drank water and thereafter, left the glass sideways, it gave me a headache. How can I accept your khādim? He will be like you."

Once, the Shaykh was inspired that there was a woman in Delhi who was very bad tempered and that if he married her, then Allāh ﷻ would raise his status in both worlds. He accepted and got married. One day a disciple came from Kabul to visit him. The Shaykh asked the disciple to bring some food from his home. He went and requested for food. The Shaykh's wife started swearing and cursing him. "Why didn't he ask for the food earlier as I have been waiting for so long? What a fraudster who fools people!" She continued talking in this manner, on and on. The disciple (out of anger) drew out a knife but then realised that this woman, after all, was his Shaykh's wife. He immediately put the knife away and remarked, "You are my Shaykh's wife, otherwise, I would have finished you off!" Then he proceeded towards the Shaykh and asked, "O Shaykh! Why have you married such an ill-mannered wife?" The Shaykh replied, "O' fool! This high status and fame that you see is due to my perseverance upon the hardship that I endure from this woman."

Damaging Effects of Extreme Anger

When a person gets angry, his behaviour becomes like a devil/Shaytān, because Shaytān is created from fire and anger is also created from fire. Sayyidunā Abū Sa'eed ؓ relates that the Messenger of Allāh ﷺ said,

اِتَّقُوا الْغَضَبَ فَإِنَّهَا جَمْرَةٌ تُوْقَدُ فِي قَلْبِ ابْنِ آدَمَ، اَلَمْ تَرَوْا اِلٰى اِنْتِفَاخِ اَوْدَاجِهٖ وَحُمْرَةِ عَيْنَيْهِ فَمَنْ اَحَسَّ مِنْ ذٰلِكَ شَيْئًا فَلْيَلْزِقْ بِالْاَرْضِ

"Save yourself from anger. Indeed, it is a hot charcoal burning in the heart of every man. Do you not see the veins of his neck swelling and the redness of his eyes? Whosoever senses anything from this should attach to the earth." (Musannaf Ibn Abi Shaiba)

The redness in the eyes indicates that there is fire there. Hence, a person should restrain his anger as much as possible. People carry out unimaginable acts due to anger which are so horrendous and despicable. Out of anger, people revolt against Allāh ﷻ and in accordance to the Islamic Laws, such a person is taken out of the fold of Islām.

Due to anger, an individual argues with his parents, a husband exceeds the limits and oppresses his wife, a wife dishonours her husband, a son disrespects his father, a student disrespects his teacher, a Mureed (disciple) disrespects his Shaykh, an Ummati (follower) disrespects his Prophet, a subject disobeys his leader and a servant disrespects Allāh ﷻ. Anger is such a destructive spiritual illness which deprives a person from affection of his elders. Tell me, if a student vents his anger towards his teacher, will the teacher show compassion towards that student? Never! We should behave respectfully towards all of our elders so that we receive their love and affection, as this love and affection is vital.

Extreme anger has destroyed thousands of families. The husband out of anger pronounces three divorces resulting in a permanent marriage breakdown. For the rest of his life, he will be regretting and his children will be cursing him as to how much of a tyrant their father was that he divorced their mother at an advanced age.

My dear friends! Anger is undoubtedly a disastrous and detrimental illness. We should not delay in seeking its remedy and restrain ourselves as much as possible when becoming angry. The Holy Prophet ﷺ said,

$$\text{لَيْسَ الشَّدِيْدُ بِالصُّرَعَةِ، إِنَّمَا الشَّدِيْدُ الَّذِيْ يَمْلِكُ نَفْسَهُ عِنْدَ الْغَضَبِ}$$

"The powerful person is not the one who overcomes his opponent but the true powerful person is the one who controls his Nafs (lower-self) at the time of anger." (Bukhārī)

Allāh's ﷻ Sustenance

Sayyidunā Mūsā عليه السلام was so strong that he once slapped a Qibti (a person from the clan of Fir'awn) which claimed his life. If his slap was so mighty, then just imagine how strong he was.

Once Sayyidunā Mūsā عليه السلام asked Allāh ﷻ how He provided suste-

| Cure for Anger | Sayyidunā Mūsā ﷺ and the Goat |

nance to the creation of the universe. Allāh ﷻ ordered him to strike a rock with his staff. Upon striking the rock, there appeared another layer and thereafter, another. After all three layers of the rock fragmented by hitting each one of them, a small insect was seen beneath the third layer eating fresh green grass. At the same time, the insect was hymning the praises of Allāh ﷻ, Subhān Allāh!

سُبْحَانَ مَنْ يَّرَانِيْ، وَيَسْمَعُ كَلَامِيْ، وَيَعْرِفُ مَكَانِيْ، وَيَذْكُرُنِيْ وَلَا يَنْسَانِيْ

"Pure is that Being Who sees me (beneath the three stones) and can hear my speech, Who knows the place of my residence. He always remembers me and never forgets me."

Sayyidunā Mūsā ؑ and the Goat

Imām Fakhrud Deen Rāzi ؒ relates an incident in his commentary, Tafseer Kabeer, that before prophethood Sayyidunā Mūsā ؑ used to graze goats and sheep. One day, a goat fled from the rest of the herd, so Sayyidunā Mūsā ؑ pursued it. However, the goat continued running for miles. Sayyidunā Mūsā's ؑ feet became soaked in blood due to the thorns and pricks and the same was the condition of the goat. Finally, when the goat became exhausted, it started to pant and eventually halted. Only then, Sayyidunā Mūsā ؑ managed to get hold of it.

What would we do in that situation? We would have slaughtered the stubborn animal, but instead what did Sayyidunā Mūsā ؑ do? Before he took out the pricks from his own feet, he took the pricks out from the feet of the goat and started to massage its feet. Then, he carried the goat on his shoulder and brought it back to its place. He did not get angry but instead he was crying and saying, "O' dear goat, if you did not have mercy on Mūsā, at least you should have had some mercy upon yourself."

The Angels observing the whole scenario, pleaded to Allāh ﷻ, "O' Allāh ﷻ, this person is worthy of Prophethood! What amazing patience, perseverance and tolerance! O' Allāh ﷻ, make him a Prophet." Allāh ﷻ replied, "I have already chosen him for Prophethood. In My infinite knowledge, he is a Prophet."

A Bedouin Urinates in the Masjid

Imām Muslim ؓ reports in his Saheeh that once a bedouin came to the Masjid and started to urinate inside. He did not know the etiquettes of the Masjid. The Sahābah ؓ immediately rushed towards him to stop him. Our Holy Prophet ﷺ said;

لَا تُزْرِمُوهُ دَعُوهُ

"Do not stop him. Leave him."

So they left him until he finished. After he finished, the Holy Prophet ﷺ summoned him and said,

إِنَّ هٰذِهِ الْمَسَاجِدَ لَا تَصْلُحُ لِشَيْءٍ مِّنْ هٰذَا الْبَوْلِ، وَلَا الْقَذَرِ إِنَّمَا هِيَ لِذِكْرِ اللهِ عَزَّ وَجَلَّ، وَالصَّلَاةِ وَقِرَاءَةِ الْقُرْآنِ

"Indeed, these Masjids are not places for urinating or for impurities. These (Masjids) are for the Dhikr of Allāh ﷻ, performing of Salāh and the recitation of the Holy Qur'ān."

Allāmah Sayyid Sulaimān Nadwi ؒ writes in his kitāb Khutubāt Madrās, that an English Historian writes, "I have not come across any person who endured so much patience, tolerance, perseverance and possessed such complete intellect like the Messenger of Islām. When a person pollutes a sanctified and sacred place of worship, usually a person becomes enraged with anger, apart from the Prophet of Islām. As a non-Muslim, I am astonished and amazed at his level of intellect and tolerance that he controlled his Nafs and at the same time, his strategy and wisdom safeguarded the whole Masjid from contaminating."

If the bedouin was stopped or driven away, it would have contaminated the whole Masjid and possibly caused physical harm to him. Subhān-Allāh! What level of tolerance!

Four Types of People

One type of people are those who become angry very quickly and let go of it very quickly. They are neither praised nor despised. A second type are those who become angry late and subdue it late, this group are also neither praised nor despised. The third type is that group of people who become angry very rarely, but when they do get angry, it is subdued very quickly. These are the best amongst us. The worst people are those who get angry very quickly but the anger prolongs with them.

Remedy for Anger

There are many remedies of anger mentioned in the Ahādeeth and in the books of our pious predecessors. Shāh Maulāna Abrārul Haque Sāhib ﷫ mentions that at the time of anger, the following things should be adhered to.

1) Recite Ta'awwudh اَعُوْذُ بِاللّٰهِ مِنَ الشَّيْطَانِ الرَّجِيْمِ.
2) Perform Wudhu.
3) If standing, then sit down. If seated, then lie down.
4) Move away from the person you become angry with or move him away from yourself.
5) Stay in the company of a pious person.
6) Engage in Dhikrullāh and recite Durood Shareef in abundance.
7) Avoid talking with the person you are angry with (for about three days).
8) Contemplate that anger will destroy my Imān like the way aloe destroys honey.
9) Remind yourself that you are a sinner in the eyes of Allāh ﷻ. If He takes you to test with your sins and mistakes, then it will be difficult for me to gain salvation. Also, by being forgiving, you have hope that Allāh ﷻ will also forgive you. Hence, to forgive is better in every aspect.
10) If any transgression is perpetrated due to anger, then pay a penalty of a sum of money or perform four Rak'ats of Salāh as an atonement.

Prescription of the Pious

One prescription is that a person recites Tasmiyah (Bismillāh) 21 times after every Salāh and blows on himself. Also, recite it three times at the time of eating and drinking and blow on the food and water. Inshā Allāh, Allāh's ﷻ mercy will manifest.

The scholars have mentioned specific names of Allāh ﷻ for specific illnesses. Hence, if someone is ill, then he should recite 'Yā Salāmu' an odd number of times then peace and tranquillity will descend. If he is in poverty, then he should recite 'Yā Mughni' then Allāh's ﷻ attribute of Ghinā (prosperity) will become manifest upon him. Likewise, by reciting يَا رَحْمٰنُ, Allāh's ﷻ attributes of mercy and benevolence will become dominant over him.

Dr Abdul-Hayy al-Ārifi ؓ, an eminent disciple of Shaykh Ashraf Ali Thānwi ؓ states that whatever the difficulty is, whether it is a debt, hardship, illness or fear of an enemy, if a person recites, يَا ذَالْجَلَالِ وَالْاِكْرَامِ 500 times, with Durood Shareef at the beginning and the end, forty days will not pass by, in which his needs will be fulfilled. This is proven from the Hadeeth in which it is mentioned that when a person calls to Allāh ﷻ with يَا أَرْحَمَ الرَّاحِمِيْنَ (O' the Most Merciful from all those who are merciful), then Allāh ﷻ sends an angel to him who says, "O' man! Allāh ﷻ, with His attribute of Mercy is focused towards you, ask for whatever you want."

Cure for Anger

Hence, by reciting this, our anger will calm down and our worldly needs will be fulfilled as well.

May Allāh ﷻ make us amongst His chosen servants, forgive our sins and cure us all from our spiritual and physical illnesses. Āmeen!

ANGER | BY DR. RAFĀQAT RASHID

Anger is a normal human emotion that everyone experiences; some more than others. As with any emotion that Allāh ﷻ has endowed mankind, each has its purpose. If it was not for the fact that man did not get angry, he would not have the capacity to defend his honour and his rights. Many of the injustices that occur in the world would not be opposed and people would cause corruption and oppression on the earth, devoid of any resistance from those they hurt. Anger has been the driving force for some of the greatest revolutions mankind has witnessed.

Anger, on the other hand if not controlled and channelled properly, can be one of the most dangerous and destructive forces witnessed. Anger has been known to destroy relationships, careers, families and even nations. This emotion is such that the person who experiences it is influenced physically, psychologically, biologically and socially.

How often does this happen to you? An event has occurred or somebody has said something which has caused you to experience the following: Your face becomes flushed, all muscles begin to tense, your eyebrows move downwards giving a fixed, serious gaze at the source or the target to which your feelings are directed, Your nostrils flare, jaws clench, your face sweats, you begin to breathe heavier, your heart begins to race, your body takes up an offensive posture, the tone of your voice becomes aggressive and loud and your pupils dilate.'

And this is just the start...what next?

1. You lose your sense of rational thinking and begin to:
    a) Shout, abuse or swear.
    b) Nonsense talk.
    c) Get physically aggressive and violent with the person or object.
    d) Make an impulsive decision which has serious implications.

2. You control your feelings and:
    a) Remain quiet.
    b) Walk away.
    c) Change the subject or calm down the situation.

Which of the above describes your reaction and how frequently do you express such emotions and actions? Are you one of those people who lose your sense of rational thinking and your anger overcomes you, or are you in control when you get angry and can bring the situation to a good end?

Modes of onset and prolongation of anger also vary with each individual. Which describes you?

   1. I get angry and irritable very quickly over the slightest thing.
   2. If I get angry, it is only for a short while.
   3. It takes a lot to get me angry.
   4. It takes me a long time to cool down.

Anger

Anger can vary from mild irritation to intense fury and rage. People generally have different levels of tolerance. Some people have a great ability to control their anger and are able to channel this anger towards something positive and beneficial, whereas others have little control. Their anger becomes a rage of impulsive behaviour that has spiralled out of control leading to a negative and destructive reaction.

Our threshold of anger can be selective to place and person. Our tolerance and reaction can vary with different individuals and settings. How best do the following statements describe you?

1. I do not express much anger to those outside my house, but I do frequently to close family members.

2. I express frequent anger both outside the house to strangers and inside the house to the family.

Some of us can behave calmly and collectively with strangers or people of high social positioning, but when we are with family and close friends, we are like raging bulls. Others fail on both accounts and are just known to be very angry and uncompromising individuals. Our environment also influences our tolerance and response. Things at work may anger us, but we do not ventilate this anger until we get home.

A person's tolerance and forbearance is an essential component of a person's outward character. Our beloved Prophet ﷺ would re-

peatedly advise the Companions ﷺ regarding this.
Sayyidunā Abū Hurairah ﷺ narrates that a man said to the Holy Prophet ﷺ, "Advise me." The Holy Prophet ﷺ said, "Do not become angry," and repeated it several times, saying, "Do not become angry." (Bukhāri)

Sayyidunā Abū Darda ﷺ narrates, "I said, 'O' Messenger of Allāh ﷺ, show me an action that will enter me into Paradise.' The Holy Prophet ﷺ said, 'Do not become angry and the Garden (Paradise) is yours.'" (Tabarāni)

It is this, coupled with nobility, generosity, modesty, humility and a nearness to Allāh ﷻ, that displays good qualities in ones character.

Sayyidunā Abdullāh Ibn Umar ﷺ asked the Holy Prophet ﷺ, "What will keep me far from the wrath of Allāh ﷻ?" The Holy Prophet ﷺ replied, "Do not be angry." (Ahmad)

Humayd Ibn Abdur-Rahmān ﷺ narrates from a Companion of the Holy Prophet ﷺ that he said, "O Messenger of Allāh ﷻ, counsel me." The Holy Prophet ﷺ said, "Do not become angry." The man said, "I reflected when the Holy Prophet ﷺ said what he said and it struck me that anger comprises all evil." (Muwatta Mālik)

There are many narrations from the Holy Prophet ﷺ which explain the evil which can ensue as a result of uncontrolled anger, as well as the evil that brings on this emotion.
Sayyidunā Abū Sa'eed al-Khudri ﷺ narrates that the Holy Prophet

ﷺ said in his Khutbah (sermon), "Certainly, anger is a burning coal in the son of Ādam's heart. Have you not seen the redness of his eyes and the swelling of his jugular veins? Whoever experiences anything of that, then let him cling to the earth." (Ahmad, Tirmizi)

It is interesting how even today, in the western world, some of the greatest philosophical writings on anger management have reference to some of Islām's classical scholars such as Imām Ghazāli ﷺ and Ibn Rushd. These scholars understood the root cause and affect of anger and wrote on this subject. The source of their work was the Holy Qur'ān and the traditions of our beloved Prophet ﷺ.

Anger is an emotion that individuals use to express that they are unhappy or irritated about a particular situation. If this emotion is controlled and used for the right reason in upholding good and shunning evil, then this emotion is praiseworthy. Good and evil is what the Holy Qur'ān and Sunnah define, not what we feel is right and wrong, as our emotion or perception of a situation may be incorrectly tuned, leading to the wrong conclusion or action. Unfortunately, many of us misunderstand this concept and feel that anger is a sign of strength and domination. Uncontrollable anger has never been a solution to any problem and has in fact, led to increased problems and destruction. True strength is not that one rages with anger when faced with a situation, for if one was confronted by someone stronger and of greater status, then that anger would diminish at first sight. Rather, true strength is that a person swallows his anger and with a steady head, deals with the situation logically.

Sayyidunā Abū Hurairah ؓ narrates that the Holy Prophet ﷺ said, "The strong man is not the one who throws others down on the ground. Rather, the strong man is he who masters himself when he is angry." (Bukhārī, Muslim)

Sayyidunā Ibn Mas'ood ؓ narrates that the Holy Prophet ﷺ said, "Whom do you reckon as the overpowering wrestler among you?" We said, "The one whom others do not wrestle to the ground." The Holy Prophet ﷺ said, "He is not that, but it is the one who masters himself when he is angry." (Muslim)

Those of us who are able to swallow our anger and forgive are the ones who become closer to Allāh ﷻ and have the most excellent of character.

"And those who when they become angry, they forgive."

(42:37)

"And those who swallow their rage and pardon people. Allāh loves the doers of good." (3:134)

Uncontrolled anger is a very common illness in today's society that affects our marriages and how we bring up our children.

So why do people get angry? Why are some people more vulnerable to uncontrollable anger compared to others? Many people throughout history have studied this subject and have come to many conclusions. Some have failed to realise the true root causes of anger and focussed on the secondary causes or external causes of anger. Rather than eliminating the root cause, their focus has been on the symptoms of anger and thus, the destructive sources of anger have not been resolved, but rather re-directed elsewhere causing damage to other aspects of the character, or just left to boil up with time, ready to explode.

Anger is a symptom of a strong emotion of displeasure caused by some type of grievance that is either real or perceived to be real by a person. As Imām Ghazāli ﷺ explains in his Ihyā, "Allāh ﷻ created the passion of anger from fire and kept it concealed in the human mind. Whenever anything stands against his wishes, anger is enhanced...the birthplace of anger is the heart." Imām Ghazāli ﷺ explains that there are 3 types of men with regards to anger:

1. No Anger - Those who have little or no anger are passive people who are like fallen leaves in the wind; they go where the wind carries them. They are weak in heart and fall prey to all nuisances. Imām Shāfi'ee ﷺ said, "He whose anger cannot be aroused is an ass."

2. Excessive Anger - This state is dangerous as such a person loses his intellect in this state and therefore, his sense of right and wrong. He no longer follows that which pleases Allāh ﷻ and falls prey to his emotions.

3. Moderate Anger - This is the praiseworthy state as such a person is no prey to other's evils and injustices and he is angry because he

hates and despises what Allāh ﷻ despises and loves what Allāh ﷻ is pleased with. Yet, when it is for worldly gains, which does not benefit his afterlife, he refrains from such anger, as this is the symptom of an ill heart.

One can therefore conclude that not all anger is unhealthy, but rather, it is a basic form of self defence that prevents us being manipulated or dominated. It is our driving force to overcome injustice and evil. If it is used in the right place, then it is praiseworthy, otherwise, it will be the source of injustice and evil. Therefore, all anger must be controlled and channelled towards righteousness. To explain the essence of the uncontrolled and blameworthy anger, I shall describe its sources as 2 types: 1) Internal inducers (root causes) and 2) External triggers (circumstantial triggers).

Kibr (Pride/Arrogance)

Certain factors affect the way we perceive our world. These causative factors are formulated in our spiritual heart (Qalb) as a result of our environment and company and then manifest themselves in our character, behaviour and our sense of logic. The scholars have labelled these as illnesses of the heart, for they have a negative affect on our spiritual self, take us away from Allāh ﷻ and make us vulnerable to the whispers of Shaytān.

According to most scholars, the root illness is pride and arrogance and from this spiritual illness, the secondary spiritual diseases develop, such as ungratefulness, miserliness, greed and jealousy etc.

Allāh ﷻ says,

$$وَإِذْ قُلْنَا لِلْمَلَائِكَةِ اسْجُدُوا لِآدَمَ فَسَجَدُوا إِلَّا إِبْلِيسَ أَبَىٰ وَاسْتَكْبَرَ وَكَانَ مِنَ الْكَافِرِينَ$$

Remember when We said to the angels: 'Prostrate yourself before Ādam,' they prostrated except Iblees; he refused and was proud and was one of the disbelievers (disobedient to Allāh)." (2:34)

Iblees was proud and arrogant and thus, when Allāh ﷻ tested him, he failed. Iblees replied and said,

$$قَالَ أَنَا خَيْرٌ مِنْهُ خَلَقْتَنِي مِنْ نَارٍ وَخَلَقْتَهُ مِنْ طِينٍ$$

"I am better than he. You created me of fire and You created him of clay." (7:12)

Iblees was jealous that Allāh ﷻ had given Ādam ؑ a higher status and ordered him and the angels to prostrate before him. Iblees therefore, objected to Allāh's ﷻ command to honour Ādam ؑ as he felt that he was more superior. Arrogance is a major illness and a sin that manifests in the form of secondary spiritual diseases. The Holy Prophet ﷺ said, "No one will enter Paradise whose heart contains an atom's weight of arrogance." (Muslim)

When a person is proud and arrogant, he believes he is far more superior and special compared to others and thus, is hurt when he sees others gain more than him, which can result in envy. He becomes greedy, miserly and has to prove himself superior by show, pomp and seeking fame. These diseases are not always obvious to him, but live in his character in some form or another. He therefore, has unreasonable expectations of others, expecting others to show respect towards him and see things the way he sees them. When things do not go along this path, then it is frustration which boils over and emerges as hate and anger. This characteristic is found in every one of us to some extent. Some more than others; the only difference is the individuals 'frustration tolerance'.

It is these internal inducers of anger which give us our irrational perceptions of reality. For example, if a person is envious (jealous) of another, then he will seek to harm him. If this is not possible, then he will become frustrated and angry, which will dominate his sense of logic and therefore, he may say something or do something that is regrettable. If someone is ungrateful of what he has, then he will take it all for granted and not appreciate its true value. Thus, if someone begins to de-value another, then he is unlikely to tolerate the other in conflict situations and so, disproportionately respond unfavourably and unjustly in a state of anger. If someone is greedy or miserly, then he will not tolerate others gaining what they have or what he has been unable to attain and therefore, his frustration may reveal itself in anger.

External Triggers of Anger

Allah ﷻ has created us all differently with different natures or temperaments. When something agrees with our nature, we embrace it, but, when it disagrees with our nature, then it becomes an irritant. It is this irritation, when it passes our individual 'frustration tolerance,' which makes us angry. Our frustration tolerance is influenced by a number of factors, which I shall also explain. To put it more simply, Islamic scholars explain three areas of personal nature that we protect and defend.

1) Material/physical needs - Our essential needs are health, food, clothes, shelter, family and loved ones. If these are threatened in anyway, our response is that of anger. This anger is praiseworthy, as long as it does not lead to transgression. We need this defence mechanism to survive. However, if these needs are not essential but are excessive or extra, like material/physical luxuries (e.g. mansion, expensive car, glamorous clothing), then to be over protective, easily irritated and to disproportionately hurt others to protect them, is a form of anger that leads to transgression. This demonstrates greed and a deep attachment to the Dunya (material world).

2) Honour/rights and dignity - To protect ones honour is an essential to survival, as long as ones self-perception is not unrealistic. If one is being unjustly treated or ridiculed, it is important to defend oneself in a dignified way. Sometimes, this may need an element of anger to motivate a response. However, if someone has self-beliefs of grandeur, which far surpass their social positioning, then this will be considered arrogance. Protecting ones rights is only righteous when it reflects the rights of others, otherwise, this is oppression and injustice. Therefore, anger stemming from such an act is not of praise.

3) Sense of values/ethics and opinions – Depending on our interests, occupation, environment and upbringing, our sense of values may differ. An Islamic scholar will give great value to books, whereas a labourer will value his tools. This sense of value is praiseworthy as long as it respects the values of others. We may also differ in our opinions on matters that do not relate directly to religion. Rather, we may differ on issue which hold some importance to us as individuals. As long as this issue is not one that displeases Allāh ﷻ, then to hold that opinion would be permissible, to the extent that we do not forcefully impose such an opinion on others, just because we feel that our opinion must prevail. This would be considered as argumentation and is a disliked trait in a character. Those who are always argumentative about their opinions, usually without any sound research, are only driving themselves to transgression. Their anger is not justified.

With due consideration to the above three areas of personal nature, our anger is only lit when we are irritated to the extent of our individual 'frustration tolerance'. This frustration tolerance is like a sliding scale which is affected by a number of factors. Those, which increase our tolerance and give us patience (Sabr) and those, which decrease our tolerance and make us easily aroused. Being happy, content, in the company of those who are patient and with good character, as well as those, whose opinion we value or those we fear, will increase our tolerance level. The following is a list of those factors that will decrease our tolerance level:

1. **Past Experiences** - Our mind is a storage of emotions related to

past experiences. Even before an incident has occurred, the mind has a tendency to predict a course of emotion and relate it to what we have learnt in the past. We may have phobias or bad experiences and thus, when an incident may lead one to experience those feelings again, one is likely to be over protective and thus, very irritable. For example, if our child is unwell and we had a past experience of another child having been admitted to hospital with a serious illness, we may feel that our doctor is not doing enough to help the recovery of our child and this may make us lose our patience.

2. **Learned Behaviour** - Behaviour can be contagious especially when it is frequently acted out before you. If parents are patient and tolerant to others, then this will reflect on their children. If the parents have an aggressive and angry nature, then this will also become the nature of their children. Our company is a very important part of who we are. This is why those who imitate the Prophet of Allāh ﷺ, the best of characters, are the best of company. Learned behaviour can also be learnt from mediums such as the TV. Watching gangster movies and violent films is portrayed onto those who watch them and they begin to emulate that behaviour in their own way.

3. **Circumstantial Vulnerabilities**- These are related to current states at the time of anger. They are usually temporary and unpredictable. Those of us who are affected by them tend to behave impulsively and suddenly sometimes, in the form of an outburst. Examples of these are:

a) Stress/Anxiety. When our stress level increases, our frustration tolerance decreases. Domestic disputes and overwork can lead to anger and irritability at work. Lack of sleep is a physical strain on the body and mind and can manifest as irritability and anger.

a) Pain. Physical and emotional pain also lowers our frustration tolerance. Somebody who has chronic pain/illness may snap at others easily. Their focus is usually on their own needs and they may feel threatened and vulnerable by those around them. This can also be the case of emotional pain such as bereavement.

c) Drugs/Alcohol/Chemical Change. Chemical imbalances of the mind can cause clouding of our logic and our emotional state, making us vulnerable and therefore, decrease our frustration tolerance. Recreational drugs/alcohol will affect our thought process and can make our behaviour erratic/clumsy and impulsive; a fuel to the process. Even a change in our hormonal balance can make us more irritable, such as in premenstrual tension.

d) Unaccomplished Expectations. We all have a general routine to the day and expect the road to be predictable. Sometimes, things do not go as they should because of delays or little mishaps. Little mishaps can be trivial on there own but if summed throughout the day, can lead to frustration. We call this "having a bad day." This is a common trigger to frustration and can spiral if not controlled. This vulnerability is usually related to ungratefulness and a disregard of the good that Allāh ﷻ has given us. It alludes to an expectation that all should be made perfect for us.

Anger and Marriage
Let us take the example of a busy housewife. The husband has not been giving her much attention; rather, he has been spending a lot of time with his work colleagues. The wife is upset and asks herself, "Why should I stay at home whilst my husband enjoys himself outside with his friends." She harbours ill-feelings towards her husband. "He doesn't take me out and rather, he prefers the company of his friends." She entertains all the negatives of her husband. She is overworked, suffering from lack of sleep and is having a bad day because she has accidently broken a vase, the washing machine is not working and her children were late for school.

Now let us look at the husband's perspective. He is late for work and has a very busy day ahead of him and is therefore quite stressed. His wife has expressed, over the last few days that she has been feeling quite upset and unloved. Her husband has been ignoring her and continuing with his work. The husband has noticed that his wife is upset, but has ignored her hoping that it will all go away. The wife's feelings remain and are not going away. In fact, they are getting worse. The husband thinks, "Why should I comfort her, she should understand that I am a busy man with deadlines." He now harbours ill-feelings towards his wife because he feels that she is ungrateful. "If she can be angry, so can I!" He has had little sleep and is quite irritable. He walks in to the kitchen, raising his voice, "Where's my breakfast." She picks up his cereal bowl and in an impulse of severe anger, screams and throws the bowl full of milk and cereal at him. For a moment, as he finds himself covered in cereal and milk, he thinks to himself. "How dare she do such a thing to me? I feed her, give her allowances and keep her and this is how she repays me. This is out of order!" In a rage, without any hesitation, he announces three divorces, only to severely regret everything moments later.

How unfortunate it is that two grown adults behave in such a way. Strong emotions can sometimes surpass our intellect and can lead to regrettable consequences. Such a situation could have been easily avoided. Chances are that the couple described, are affectionate to each other, but they have let circumstantial hiccups break up their understanding and resolve.

Negative reactions such as these are a result of over-emotion, pride and arrogance, the root cause of such an unfortunate ending. Arrogance manifests in individuals in different ways in the form of secondary spiritual diseases, such as ungratefulness, greed, jealousy, feelings of superiority etc. It is this arrogance that demands that others comply with me. The perception becomes self-centred and selfish, with little thought given to the feelings of others. The person becomes irritated, if things do not go according to their wishes. The frustration tolerance of the individual will dictate the intensity and speed of onset of anger as this level of irritation magnifies. The lower the frustration tolerance, the faster the onset of anger and the higher the amplitude of the reaction, like a fierce wave which then falls, only to leave destruction.

Many marriages are destroyed because of this anger. Couples fail to tolerate each other and so, irritate each other even in the slightest, irrelevant things. When a marriage breaks, many are affected; the couple, children, the couple's parents, relatives and friends. The children are severely emotionally scarred. An Exeter study in 1994 by Cockett & Tripp, showed that "Children in 're-ordered families' (i.e divorced families) suffered problems of adjustment until later in life. These poor children wanted to stay with both natural parents even with the tensions involved." How sad it is when children would rather live in an unpleasant house with constant feuding between parents, than live with one parent alone, away from feuds. Anger in a marriage is no trivial thing. Such feelings, if actioned beyond proportion, can lead to serious consequences.

Virtues of Marriage

Our frustration tolerance varies with different individuals and different places. It may be that when we are at work, this frustration tolerance may be high with colleagues or the boss. We become very tolerant and not easily aroused, but when we are at home with our husband/wife, our frustration tolerance is low and even the slightest thing can change our anger. It is as if we have a split personality. The difference between home and outside the home are the people and not the place. It is surprising how quickly our behaviour or personality can change with different people. A husband may be shouting at his wife one moment and answering his mobile with a pleasant tone the next. How easily and swiftly he is able to change the tone of his language in such a situation, no matter how angry he may be with his wife, yet no such effort is made to resolve disputes with his wife with such pleasant words.

We do not want to look like fools at work by losing our temper all the time, yet when we are at home it is not an issue. Does this mean that we are not as concerned about our husband's/wife's perception of us, as compared to our boss or colleagues? If we think the opinions and feelings of our boss or friends are more important than those of our husband/wife, then we do not really appreciate the value of our husband/wife. This is not to say that we do not love our husband/wife or care about them, rather, we do not value them the way they should be valued.

The main reason we do not value our husband/wife is because we are unable to understand the purpose and virtues of married life. Responsibility towards fulfilling each others rights and valuing each other is considered a burden because of the lack of understanding we have in appreciating the purpose of marriage. The burden only exists because we fail to see the benefits in married life. This failure to see the benefits of married life is what leads to intolerance. On the other hand, if the couple appreciate why they are together and what purpose they serve themselves, their children, family and society, they will overlook unpleasant situations and circumstances and remain together, not only to fulfil their sexual urge, but also to lead a life which provides security and comfort for both of them as well as their children. An unfortunate trend in today's society is that pre-marital experimentation is considered a better and safer way of choosing a husband/wife. The one, most severe evil that results from this is that this experimentation becomes more of an avenue for relief of immoral desires than a means or a purpose in the search for a suitable husband/wife, especially for the promiscuous men, who use women as an ego boost to uphold their rank with their peers rather than to start a family.

Allāh ﷻ describes one of the essential purposes of married life that, *"...They are your garments and you are their* **garments."** (2:187)

The purpose of garments is to *protect* one from extremes of temperature, to provide a covering which *conceals* essential aspects of the body that are personal and to provide modesty for the purpose of dignity and honour. Likewise, husband and wife *protect* and help each other in times of physical and emotional lows by consoling each other and *concealing* each others faults from others. They are a demonstration of honour and dignity if they fulfil the rights accorded to each other.

Marriage is to build a family atmosphere, which is supportive, gives one a sense of belonging, importance, responsibility and maturity and provides comfort in the time of need. Couples with a happy home are more empowered and work more efficiently than those who have a broken home and a stressful home environment. Marriage imparts values of mercy and compassion in individuals and provides a base where they can return to energise and enjoy tranquility. Allāh ﷻ, Most High, says in the Holy Qur'ān:

وَمِنْ آيَاتِهِ أَنْ خَلَقَ لَكُم مِّنْ أَنفُسِكُمْ أَزْوَاجًا لِّتَسْكُنُوا إِلَيْهَا وَجَعَلَ بَيْنَكُم مَّوَدَّةً وَرَحْمَةً إِنَّ فِي ذَٰلِكَ لَآيَاتٍ لِّقَوْمٍ يَتَفَكَّرُونَ

"Among His signs is that He has created spouses for you among yourselves so that you may dwell in tranquility with them, and He has planted love and mercy between you. In that are signs for people who reflect." (30:21)

When one has a happy home, he can appreciate the blessings of Allāh ﷻ. He becomes thankful and fulfils half the responsibilities that Islām demands of him in this world of worshipping Allāh ﷻ by fulfilling his obligations and abstaining from sin. "When the servant of Allāh ﷻ marries, he has fulfilled half the (responsibilities laid on him by the) faith." (Mishkāt)

The essential ingredients in building a happy home, so that the fruits of married life become wholesome, is to acknowledge and value each others rights. Before I go into the subject of rights between husband and wife, it is important to understand the general disposition of man and woman; only then will one appreciate how they complement each other. Today's society limits men and women only to physical differences that are clearly visible and fails to see that the emotional liability and the psychological characteristics also vary between the two genders.

Understanding the Disposition of Men and Women: An Aid to Anger Resolution in a Marriage

Equality of the Sexes
Men and women are quiet different. There are those differences which are obvious, such as the physical differences like body size,

musculature, strength and physical stamina. There are also the obvious emotional or psychological differences that exist between men and women, which we all recognise and understand. Then, there are those subtle differences that exist in the psychological make-up of men and women that we do not fully understand. For example, why is it that more women tend to be nurses or infant school teachers? Why is it that more women take up secretarial and administration positions than men? Why is it that men take on more leadership roles or more physically demanding roles? Is this because of male dominance, as the feminists seem to argue, or is it because those roles are compatible with the natural characteristics of that gender?

I suppose the feminists do have a point with their claim that the majority of history has been dominated by men who have developed a subordinated role for women and so, the distinct individual characteristics and quality of men and women cannot be accurately assessed from a solely historical account. Being able to recognise the distinction between men and women is important because it is only when we recognise the strengths, qualities and abilities of each gender that we will appreciate and respect the importance of their role to greater society.

We cannot conclude that one gender is more superior to the other and so, advocate the superior gender. A cricket manager will identify the strengths and weaknesses of his players and assign each player a position relative to this. This is not to say that one cricketer is more superior to another, but rather, that each is suited for a role that complements his strengths and weaknesses and thus, enhances effective team work. Some of the players will be good batters and others will be good ballers; each has a role that complements the other and enhances the team. It may be that one has a strength that is a weakness in another and vice versa. In a similar way, the value of a woman is equal to that of a man, even though they are different in gender.

In today's liberalist concept of equality of the sexes as a component of political correctness, this recognition of the distinction between the male and female, and thus, respect for gender, is diminishing. The further we push for the modern day concept of equality in gender, as a principle of political correctness, the more we lose our awareness of those characteristics that make men and women important. I do not claim that equality of gender is a bad thing, what I do claim is that I disagree with the modern day equality of gender that seems to drive women to become men because the role of men is unadmittedly considered a superior role, even by the feminists (Wollstonecraft, p.117). This is not respect for womanhood, but rather, a principle that demeans the quality and the status of being a mother or a wife. It is an advocation to a social imbalance of the fundamental foundations of the family and thus, society and nation.

Women are moving away from the motherly/domestic roles and taking up careers as a matter of priority. The role of mother and wife are seen as inferior roles. Succesful career women who have forsaken the role of mother and wife, are seen as the role models for women today. My claim is not that a career is a bad thing, but rather, if women are driven to leave the domestic role, then who will replace them; the men, nursery nurses, child minders? There goes the importance of maternal-child bonding and intimacy which are undoubtedly, essential ingredients in nurturing children. (see: Ruddick, *Maternal Thinking*, 1989)

The Difference between Men and Women

Dr Michael Conner, a clinical, medical and family psychologist, having analysed years of research on understanding the difference between men and women, concludes that there are some vital differences that are observed between men and women which play a fundamental role in the strengths and weaknesses men and women possess. Conner's claim is that women differ from men, in that they are as different from each other psychologically as they are physically. I will summarise the differences in three general sub-headings, so one can understand and appreciate the distinction between the genders. (Conner, M.G.)

1.   Approach to Problem Solving and Thinking

Both genders are similarly effective in resolving problems but they differ in their approach and therefore, may produce different results. Women tend to explore problems with sometimes different considerations which revolve around discussing and negotiating and trying to amalgamate all responses as a final solution. The methodology of solving is more important than the actual resolution. Women will be more inclined towards an all inclusive based approach on character, trust and co-operation. (Beuchamp, p.371).

Their thoughts are more intertwined with other considerations and therefore, can be overwhelming and their view on things can seem to be of greater complexity and can sometimes, seem less clear. They may find it harder to separate their personal experience and emotion from the problem.

For men, a difference exists in that they are not as focussed in combining others accounts in their considerations and their approach is more a drive to an answer that seems right rather than an approach that seems right. For this reason, their approach is a more demonstrative approach where a resolution must be reached as a show or demonstration of their competence. For this reason, the male approach is a more authoritative and less 'beating around the bush' approach. A group of men will resolve problems by appointing a leader and work through a command based approach using principles and rules with an emphasis on rights and obligations. Men have a greater ability to separate personal experience and emotion from problems and thus, reduce complexities that hinder a quick resolution. Their approach is less inter-dependent of other considerations and focussed in a sequential way.

2. Memory and Sensitivity

Men recall information in a very structured, activity based way. Their memory tends to be more a construct of experiences related to physical activity and challenging tasks. Women recall information with a strong emotional component. Just as a certain fragrance or a certain landscape may make us feel good, in women, this is enhanced more so than men. Certain thoughts, smells and situations may arouse a sensitive aspect of memory which may be overwhelmed with emotion. Women are more likely to be sensitive and emotional as a result. The hormonal variation between the genders has a substantial effect on personal sensitivities. Testosterone in men has a desensitising effect, which reduces emotional dependence and empathy. The oestrogen and progesterone levels in women have the opposite effect and can cause increasing sensitivities and emotion. Hence, the menstrual cycle can arouse emotional states in some women.

3. Communication

A man's preference of approach to communication and intimacy is a more physically based one. They relate and bond more with physical activities such as sports, competition and sexual activities. Their response is more in tune with sharing tasks, distinct goals and sequential reasoning which is non-complex. A woman's preference of approach to communication and intimacy is a more dialogue based one. Their response is more in tune with sharing of experience, emotion and intimate verbal communication and flattery. Many men find this form of intimacy uncomfortable and intense.

Women tend to use the right side of the brain more than men. The right side of the brain is more in tune with understanding emotion, expressions and gestures and for this reason, a woman is more connected with her inner feelings and more aware of other's gestures. This is suitable for her as a mother, as mothers are more aware of infant gestures than fathers and are more tolerable and yet sensitive to a child's needs. Men are not as connected with the right side of the brain and are therefore, more tuned in with the left, which is the side related to logic, calculation and concrete thinking. Men can therefore, think more without the emotional or lateral complexities and thus, can be more focussed on action rather than being overwhelmed with the intricacies. For this reason, they may be more assertive and have higher self-esteem because they can action their choices without the complexities. (Feingold, p.429)

Accepting Differences in Gender: An Essential to Conflict Resolution

These differences between men and women are what makes it sometimes difficult for one to understand the other. It is not always easy for a man to feel emotional and yet at the same time, express it in the way that a woman expresses such emotions. Women are more likely to communicate their emotions and may find it easier to express them than men. This has its advantages in that, women are able to express an emotional state better than men, but it also has its disadvantages in that, it may make the women more vulnerable to be so open in expression.

Men do not tend to show empathy as much as women towards others and can therefore, seem ignorant or deliberately cold-hearted. Even if they do, it may not have an overwhelming effect as much as it would for women. Men tend to be seen as emotionally detached, which can sometimes cause conflict between husband and wife. I am not supporting the idea that this is an excuse for men to behave in such a way; far from it! Rather, a man must learn to show more empathy as this behaviour can also be partly acquired. An empathy block is likely to infuriate the wife as it gives the impression that, "I dont care!". What is required is a genuine attitude which demonstrates that, "I do care, but I am not sure how to show it!"

The truth of the matter is that men and women must learn to accept their differences. The wife must understand that the husband is not always as emotionally attached and able to show intimate affection like she can but she can help him express these elemental ingredients in their marriage. The husband must understand that his wife has over-sensitivities and emotional vulnerabilities and he must understand that this is not intentional. Each has to understand that there are differences of perception and expression. They should not frustrate themselves and behave indecently or aggressively with the other when the other does not comply. Rather, they should compromise.

A man has the upperhand in forcing his opinions on his wife because he is physically stronger and can demand rights forcefully. This is not always the case for the wife and this pressure of conforming to the husbands expectations or opinions is what breaks her. Sayyidunā Abū Hurairah ؓ reported that the Messenger of Allāh ﷺ said: "Take my advice with regard to women: Act kindly towards women, for they were created from a rib and the most crooked part of a rib is its uppermost. If you attempt to straighten it, you will break it and if you leave it alone, it will remain crooked; so act kindly towards women." (Bukhāri and Muslim)

Some men misunderstand this Hadeeth and use it as amunition against their wives; claiming that their wife is a crooked rib! This is wrong and is a failure of understanding the wisdom of what is meant here. This Hadeeth is a solution to domestic conflict. Look how beautifully the Messenger of Allāh ﷺ advised the men regarding their wives. He says that you should behave kindly towards them because being kind is to reason with them without overwhelming them with negative emotion. Rather, you should encourage positive emotion where they are likely to be more attentive and comply. In simple words, the Messenger of Allāh ﷺ describes the female personality as one which is not rational like men's. Men cannot always make sense of it because their perceptions and approach are different and not as complex and intertwined in emotion as women. To men, the personality characteristics of a woman are not always linear or follow a predictable course which men appreciate between themselves. Thus, they can seem unpredictable to them or irrational. A rib is such that it is not straight but uniformly bends (a predicatable course) and as we get to the uppermost part, it becomes the most crooked; the bend becomes increasingly so compared to the rest, which was unpredictable (beyond male understanding). When the husband fails to understand his wife's reaction, he should not confront her and force her to think or behave the way he wants her to behave, as this is only going to break her and destroy their relationship and marriage.

Protecting the Gaze

قُلْ لِلْمُؤْمِنِينَ يَغُضُّوا مِنْ أَبْصَارِهِمْ وَيَحْفَظُوا فُرُوجَهُمْ ذَٰلِكَ أَزْكَىٰ لَهُمْ إِنَّ اللَّهَ خَبِيرٌ بِمَا يَصْنَعُونَ

"Say to the believing men to lower their gazes and protect their private parts; that is purer for them. Verily, Allāh is fully aware of what they do." (24:30)

Introduction

My dear brothers and sisters, Allāh ﷻ, through His infinite mercy has given us a religion which is complete and accomplished. He has clearly explained to us the do's and dont's in our everyday lives so that we can become successful in both worlds. Islām has the solution to all our problems and difficulties. It is our responsibility to find the cure and solution.

In this day and age, due to the high immodesty and shamelessness which has spread through the vast media, internet and billboards, many people's lives have been destroyed. Our brothers and sisters have ruined their lives in fornication, adultery, masturbation and in viewing pornography on the internet. Lifelong marriages have been broken due to unlawful love affairs. On a social level our society has been plagued with huge problems such as rape, prostitution, child molestation, AIDS and other sexually transmitted diseases.

The question arises as to what is the root of all these problems? Our elders and pious predecessors, who looked at the world with the eye of the heart, with the insight, enlightened and illuminated by the light of the Holy Qur'ān and Ahādeeth, have diagnosed all these spiritual illnesses to be brought about by one deadly disease. The root of all these illnesses and problems is the sin of the eyes, casting evil glances and looking at Ghair Mahram (strange men/women) with lustful gazes. Unfortunately, today we do not even consider casting evil glances to be a sin, when in reality, it is the root of numerous vices and sins.

In Sūrah An-Noor, Allah ﷻ orders the believers to lower their gazes and guard their private parts:

$$قُل لِّلْمُؤْمِنِينَ يَغُضُّوا مِنْ أَبْصَارِهِمْ وَيَحْفَظُوا فُرُوجَهُمْ ذَٰلِكَ أَزْكَىٰ لَهُمْ ۗ إِنَّ اللَّهَ خَبِيرٌ بِمَا يَصْنَعُونَ$$

"Say to the believing men to lower their gazes and protect their private parts; that is purer for them. Verily, Allāh is fully aware of what they do." (24:30)

Avenues of Sin

The beauty of our religion Islām, is that it strictly prohibits and controls all those channels, means and avenues leading to the sin. For example, where Islām has forbidden the consumption of alcohol, it has not stopped at only making drinking of alcohol prohibited. Rather, to reinforce the prohibitions, it has ruled on so many avenues associated with alcohol. For example, the manufacturing, transporting, handling, selling and serving of alcohol are all forbidden, just as the drinking of alcohol is prohibited.

People used to worship the sun at fixed times. Accordingly, even performance of Salāh at sunrise, zenith (noon) and sunset have been prohibited, in order for us to dispel any notion to an onlooker of sun worship. Although the performer of Salāh is not worshipping the sun, nevertheless, the remotest resemblance of this has been removed.

Avenues of Adultery and Fornication

Adultery is an extremely grave sin about which the Holy Qur'ān warns;

$$وَلاَ تَقْرَبُوا الزِّنٰى اِنَّهُ كَانَ فَاحِشَةً$$

"Do not even go near to adultery, indeed it is a shameless act." (17:32)

Islām has restricted all avenues which lead to adultery. For example, the intermingling of non-Mahram men and women unnecessarily and the emergence of Muslim ladies without Hijāb to the extent that, they have been instructed to remain within their homes. When a genuine need arises to emerge, then it is permissible with full Hijāb and modesty and concealing ones beauty. Even the wearing of noisy jewellery is banned. Why? The sound of jewellery is enough to instigate desires in a person. Similarly, the applying of strong perfume is forbidden. It appears in a Hadeeth of Tirmizi that the Holy Prophet ﷺ said, "A woman who emerges outside applying perfume and passes by men is an adulteress." (Tirmizi)

Men are instructed, whenever a genuine need arises to communicate with Ghair Mahram women, that this should be done by lowering the gaze and protecting the modesty. All these instructions are given to prevent the ultimate act of adultery. Hence, Islām restricts all avenues which lead to sins.

Wisdom behind the Verses of Sūrah An-Noor

Coming back to the verses of Sūrah An-Noor mentioned earlier, Allāh ﷻ addresses our beloved Prophet ﷺ by instructing him,

$$\text{قُل لِّلْمُؤْمِنِينَ يَغُضُّوا مِنْ أَبْصَارِهِمْ وَيَحْفَظُوا فُرُوجَهُمْ ذَٰلِكَ أَزْكَىٰ لَهُمْ إِنَّ اللَّهَ خَبِيرٌ بِمَا يَصْنَعُونَ}$$

"Say to the believing men to lower their gazes and protect their private parts; that is purer for them. Verily, Allāh is fully aware of what they do." (24:30)

Why did Allāh ﷻ not directly instruct the Ummah to lower their gazes in the same way that He directly ordered us to establish Salāh, discharge Zakāt, observe Fast and perform Hajj etc? Why did He make the Holy Prophet ﷺ a medium to order us? Shaykh Hakeem Akhtar Sāhib ﷫ explains this beautifully as follows, "Sometimes, a modest father feels embarrassed and ashamed of directly speaking to his son regarding a particular shameful matter. Hence, he assigns his close friend to put the delicate and shameful matter to his son. Likewise, Allāh ﷻ is modest and being a shameful act, He instructs His beloved to tell His bondsmen to lower their gazes." Subhān-Allāh!

First Stage - Protecting the Gaze

The first stage is protecting and safeguarding ones gaze. If this is adhered to, then a person will never be involved in adultery. The

Hadeeth Qudsi of Tabarāni says, "The lustful gaze is an arrow from the arrows of Shaytān. Whosoever, on account of My fear forgoes it, I shall transform it into such sweetness which he will experience in his heart." (Tabarāni)

In another Hadeeth, the Holy Prophet ﷺ says, "The eyes too commit adultery and their adultery is to view (Ghair Mahram)." (Mishkāt)

Bounty of Vision

Let us reflect upon the structure, mechanism amd functioning of this eyesight which Allāh ﷻ has bestowed upon us. From birth until death it operates without servicing or effort for free. It allows you to view any item you choose. However, the day, Allāh ﷻ forbid, some problem with our vision is experienced, a tremor runs throughout our bodies. What if we were to lose our eyesight?

A person who has vision problems is prepared to spend his entire wealth to have it restored. Even a weakening of eyesight, double vision, flickering, squinting or cross-eye is enough to send us rushing to the opticians in an attempt to have this defect corrected. However, this priceless bounty, which is granted to us from birth until death, is an unbelievably complex organ, working automatically without any input from us. Moreover, it is probably the most sensitive organ in our body. One notices whenever a piece of grit or speck of dust enters the eye, what discomfort, panic, anxiety and pain this causes.

The eyes have been perfectly located in the human body and protected on all sides by a defence system. A complex bone structure surrounds it on all sides; thereafter, eye-brows and finally eye-lashes. All this is encapsulated in a face of immense beauty. This is such an outstanding bounty from Allāh ﷻ without any effort on our part. All we are asked to do is use it in an appropriate manner. We are only forbidden to employ it in those areas wherein lies our own spiritual destruction. We just need to save ourselves from viewing two things:

(1) Ghair Mahrams (people whom it is permissible for us to marry),
(2) Any person with contempt in our heart.

These are the only two restrictions being applied. We are free to view everything else.

Reward for Viewing Certain Things

There are some things which we are not only allowed to view, but we gain tremendous reward for viewing them. When one of us views his parents with the gaze of love and affection, Allāh ﷻ grants this person the reward of one Hajj and one Umrah. Similarly, when we view the Holy Ka'bah we will have Allāh ﷻ bestowing His infinite mercy upon us. This also applies to viewing the Book of Allāh ﷻ, the Holy Qur'ān.

Furthermore, when a person views his or her spouse with love and affection, then Allāh ﷻ looks upon both of them with His Mercy.

For this reason, the Scholars of Tafseer have mentioned that Allāh ﷻ has used the words "مِنْ أَبْصَارِهِمْ" meaning lower some of your gaze. The word 'min' has been used to imply that not all your gaze should be lowered. It is only when there is a Ghair Mahram present, otherwise we should raise our gaze to view those things which will bring us tremendous rewards as mentioned. Allāh ﷻ invites us to view the earth, heavens, skies, mountains, rivers, orchards etc, in order to increase our gratitude for Him and value His bounties and favours.

If we protect our eyes from lustful glances, we are promised the taste of the sweetness of Imān. Once the sweetness of Imān enters the heart, it will never be taken back. Thus, by protecting the eyes, one is given glad tidings of a good death.

The Holy Prophet ﷺ said, "Verily, the evil glance is a poisonous arrow from the arrows of Iblees. For he who abstains from casting evil glances, I will grant such Imān **that he will feel the sweetness of it in his heart.**" Hāfiz Ibn Katheer ؒ mentions in his Tafseer, "for him who protects his eyes from unlawful gazes, Allāh ﷻ will grant the light of the heart."

Imām Wāqidi ؒ and many other historians have related a historical incident during the Caliphate of Sayyidunā Umar ؓ. This incident will open our eyes to the status of the noble Companions ؓ and to what extent they acted upon the order of protecting the gaze.

The Muslims, under the leadership of Sayyidunā Abū Ubaidah Ibn Jarrāh ⚜, had surrounded a Roman fort and stronghold in Shām (Syria). However, the siege dragged on for some considerable time. When the Romans realised the Muslims were not shifting or giving up, they concocted a strategy. They sent a message to Sayyidunā Abū Ubaidah Ibn Jarrāh ⚜ notifying him of their decision to surrender and allow the Muslim army to enter through the city gates, march through the mall containing shops and up to the Royal Palace. Meanwhile, they drew up a strategy. Being aware of the long time that the Muslim army had been away from their home towns and their wives, they encouraged all the young maidens of the locality to dress up elegantly and stand outside seductively and provocatively, along the mall with a view to divert the Muslim soldiers and distract them towards rape, loot and chaos. This would weaken their spirit and Imān and would give the Roman army an opportunity to attack them from the rear and defeat the Muslims.

Spiritual Insight of Sayyidunā Abū Ubaidah ⚜

When Muslims practice upon their Deen, Allāh ﷻ grants spiritual vision and insight (Firāsat). Our pious predecessors have said,

$$اِتَّقُوْا مِنْ فِرَاسَةِ الْمُؤْمِنِ فَاِنَّهُ يَنْظُرُ بِنُوْرِ اللهِ$$

"Be alert to the insight of the Mu'min,
he views with the Noor (light) of Allāh."

When the Roman terms of surrender were read out to Sayyidunā Abū Ubaidah ⚜ he became suspicious. Until now, they fiercely resisted and all of a sudden, they wished to surrender and even open the main gates, allowing them to march un-opposed along the mall to the Royal Palace! Nevertheless, he accepted the surrender and then summoned his entire army of a few thousand soldiers to deliver a sermon.

"It is only the Favours and Grace of Allāh ﷻ that the enemy have surrendered and are inviting us to enter the city. You should surely enter, however, I wish to recite a verse of the Holy Qur'ān unto you which you should act upon as you enter:

$$\text{قُلْ لِلْمُؤْمِنِيْنَ يَغُضُّوْا مِنْ اَبْصَارِهِمْ وَيَحْفَظُوْا فُرُوْجَهُمْ ذٰلِكَ اَزْكٰى لَهُمْ اِنَّ اللّٰهَ خَبِيْرٌ بِمَا يَصْنَعُوْنَ}$$

Say to the believing men that they should lower their gazes and protect their private parts; that is purer for them. Verily, Allāh is fully aware of what they do. (24:30)

Accordingly, the entire army entered the city, reciting this verse and looking down at their feet. Not one individual raised his gaze to look around at the lure of the seductive and beautiful young girls on either side.

Amazed and baffled, all the residents of the city exclaimed with one voice, "What creation is this?" because usually an army which enters a city victorious, commences with havoc and anarchy. Many of the onlookers accepted Islām witnessing this spectacle. Subhān-Allāh! Just ponder over the incident and let us reflect upon how

Allāh ﷻ made the Sahābah ؓ successful in this world and the Hereafter.

An Amazing Incident

An amazing incident is mentioned in 'At-Targheeb Wat-Tarheeb' which shows that there are some courageous servants of Allāh ﷻ who, when confronted by such events where his or her chastity or modesty are tested, they choose to save themselves. Thus, Allāh ﷻ honoured them and elevated their ranks in both worlds.

There was a young man whose body and clothes always radiated with fragrance of musk and amber. A colleague commented, "You are an amazing fellow, spending such large amounts on top quality perfumes and fragrances. Everytime we meet, some aroma radiates from you."

The man replied, "By Allāh ﷻ! I have not spent a penny on perfumes or fragrance!"

"Then where does this scent come from?!"

"That is a secret, which I do not wish to divulge."

"No, you must tell me!" Man yearns for what is prohibited unto him! It is a trait of man to hanker after something which is prohibited. Accordingly, this friend insisted upon the secret, whereupon, the young man related:

Amazing Incident

"I worked in my father's household store. One day an old woman purchased a lot of goods and requested my father to instruct me to carry them to her home and collect the payment. I left with her and arrived at her residence which was a huge mansion. We entered a grand living room, wherein, a young beautiful woman was sitting upon a couch.

Upon observing me, she came across, grabbed my hand and started pulling me towards the couch. Agitated and perplexed, I tried to move away, but she kept pulling and seducing me.

The only thing that came to my mind was to make an excuse to visit the lavatory. She instructed her servants to clean the toilet before I entered. I relieved myself and took my own faeces and rubbed it all over my clothes and body to make myself appear disgusting and unappealing. As soon as I reappeared, she flew into a rage and shouted to her maid-servants to return this mad man where he came from!

I had one dirham in my pocket with which I purchased some soap and lowered myself into the river to clean my clothes and body as best as possible. That night when I retired to bed, I saw an angel in a human form in my dream. He said, 'I have been sent by Allāh ﷻ to give you glad tidings of Paradise in return of your saviour from sin.' Thereafter he applied some fragrance to my clothes and body and said, 'For the way you applied faeces to protect yourself from sin, you are being rewarded.' From that morning, until this day, the aroma and scent remains with me." Subhān-Allāh!

A Second Amazing Incident

Imām Ghazāli ﷺ has related in 'Ihyā-ul-Uloom', the episode of a Tābi'ee, Sulaimān Ibn Yasār ﷺ, an extremely knowledgeable and handsome scholar who lived in Madeenah Munawwarah and who during his childhood, served the mothers of the believers, Maimoonah ﷺ and Ā'ishah ﷺ.

Once, he departed for Makkah with a companion for Hajj. Along the route, they camped at Abwa. His companion went to the local village to purchase some food. The place they had camped was overlooked by a hill, upon which were Bedouin houses. From here emerged an extremely beautiful woman, who upon observing Sulaimān Ibn Yasār ﷺ below, became infatuated with him and came down to seduce him.

She removed her Niqāb and appeared as beautiful as the full moon. As she spoke, Sulaimān Ibn Yasār ﷺ mistook her to be a beggar asking for food. As he hurried to find something for her, she spoke, "I am not in need of food, rather, I seek from you what a woman seeks from a man!" Sulaimān Ibn Yasār ﷺ replied, "Shaytān has sent you here!" He then placed his head between his knees and began to cry profusely. Afraid at being apprehended or disgraced, the Bedouin woman left hurriedly.

Sulaimān's ﷺ companion now returned from the village and as he arrived he noticed Sulaimān's ﷺ face and eyes reddened. He inquired, "What is the matter?!" "Nothing, I remembered my wife and children." "No, it is something else; your condition testifies to it!" Upon his companion's insistence, Sulaimān ؑ related what had happened. Hearing this episode, his companion began to cry. Sulaimān ؑ inquired, "Brother, why do you cry?" He replied, "It is Allāh's ﷻ grace and favour that I was not in your position, for I would undoubtedly, have become submerged in sin under such circumstances. I cry out of gratefulness to Allāh ﷻ."

Thereafter, they proceeded for Hajj, arrived in Makkah, performed Tawāf and sat in meditation between Maqām Ibrāheem and Hajr-Aswad. Due to tiredness, Sulaimān ؑ fell into slumber and dreamt of Sayyidunā Yūsuf ؑ, extremely handsome and young.

Sulaimān ؑ asked him, "Who are you?" The man replied, "I am Yūsuf." Sulaimān ؑ inquired, "Yūsuf the Siddeeq (truthful)?" He said, "Yes!" Sulaimān ؑ commented, "Your episode with Zulaikha is truly amazing!" Sayyidunā Yūsuf ؑ replied, "Your episode with the Bedouin woman from Abwa is even more amazing!"

The Holy Prophet's ﷺ Compassion with a Young Companion

We need to realise the grave consequences of these lustful gazes and restrain our eyes from prohibited things. Let me share with you, an incident from the time of the Holy Prophet ﷺ which will primarily, exhibit the compassion of the Holy Prophet ﷺ and secondly, instil in us the reality of this spiritual illness of our lustful gazes. Hopefully, it will open our eyes and minds.

Once, a young man visited the Holy Prophet ﷺ and requested, "O Rasūlullāh ﷺ! Grant me permission to fornicate." Observe the kindness and affection of our beloved Prophet ﷺ, for if somebody was to come to us and speak in this manner, we would belittle, scold and rebuke them. The Holy Prophet ﷺ seated him down and explained, "Tell me, this act of fornication which you are proposing, will it be with some woman?" "Yes." Rasūlullāh ﷺ commented, "If somebody was to perform such an act with your sister, will you find it acceptable?" "No, Never!" the young man replied. Rasūlullāh ﷺ continued, "If somebody was to act in this manner with your mother, will you find it acceptable?" "No, Never!" the young man replied. The Holy Prophet ﷺ then asked, "With your maternal aunt?" "No, Never!" the young man replied. The Holy Prophet ﷺ continued, "With your paternal aunt?" "No, Never!" the young man replied.

The Holy Prophet ﷺ finally commented, "The person with whom you wish to act in this manner will undoubtedly be somebody's sister, mother, maternal aunt or paternal aunt." Immediately the man replied, "I will not act in this manner." Thereafter, the Holy Prophet ﷺ placed his blessed hand on the young man's chest and supplicated, "O Allāh! Remove the dirt and filth from his heart."

The Sahābi ؓ who narrated this episode says, "After this incident, the young man's gaze always remained lowered." This was the blessings of the Du'ā of the Holy Prophet ﷺ. Any person with a certain degree of morals will not tolerate any stranger gazing at his wife, sister, daughter, mother or aunt, so likewise, if we perpetrate this sinful act of the lustful gaze, then the husband of this woman, or the brother of this woman, or the father of this woman, or the son of this woman, or the nephew of this woman, will definitely dislike and detest this act. Let us make a firm resolution to adhere to the teachings of our Holy Prophet ﷺ. Let us supplicate to Allāh ﷻ to safeguard our eyes from perpetrating the lustful gazes.

Four Avenues of Attack

The great scholar, Shaykh Ashraf Ali Thānwi ؒ states, "When Allāh ﷻ rejected Shaytān from Paradise and condemned him, he boldly and arrogantly exclaimed, 'When you have thrown me out of Paradise and accepted my Du'ā of a life until the Day of Judgement, then I will lay await to deviate the children of Ādam, who was the cause of my rejection in this way.' He said,

قَالَ فَبِمَآ اَغْوَيْتَنِيْ لَاَقْعُدَنَّ لَهُمْ صِرَاطَكَ الْمُسْتَقِيْمَ ثُمَّ لَاٰتِيَنَّهُمْ مِّنْ بَيْنِ اَيْدِيْهِمْ وَمِنْ خَلْفِهِمْ وَعَنْ اَيْمَانِهِمْ وَعَنْ شَمَآئِلِهِمْ وَلاَ تَجِدُ اَكْثَرَهُمْ شٰكِرِيْنَ

"Now You have led me astray, I will certainly sit for them (in ambush) on Your straight path. Then I will come upon them from their front side, from their rear, from their right and from their left and you will not find most of them grateful." (7:16-17)

Shaykh Ashraf Ali Thānwi ؒ comments, "Shaytān forgot to mention two directions: from above and below. Hence, he ambushes from four sides. However, protection is either from above or below. So establish a relationship with Allāh ﷻ above; incline towards Him and seek His assistance. Thereafter, keep your gaze lowered; Allāh ﷻ will keep you protected."

A lustful gaze creates havoc spiritually. Moreover, it is so rampant in our society that perchance, there may be only one or two who are saved from this malady. All around us we are surrounded by the call to view, to stare, to glance, or to gaze. Allāh ﷻ says,

$$يَعْلَمُ خَائِنَةَ الْأَعْيُنِ وَمَا تُخْفِي الصُّدُورُ$$

"He knows the treachery of the eyes and whatever is concealed by hearts." (40:19)

In this verse, Allāh ﷻ mentions two sins which people consider trivial or minor. The two sins implied here are immoral gazing and incorrect intention. We dismiss these sins as trivial and small and do not attach any importance to refrain from them. Other sins of the ears, mouth, hands or feet are noticeable by people, hence, a person refrains from them due to the possibility of others finding out and his honour being blemished. However, with the lustful gaze, after perpetrating the act, a person still remains in his position; a scholar remains a scholar, Hāji Sāhib remains Hāji Sāhib etc. If an educated or professional person ogles, he remains educated. No difference arises in his profession and no disgrace is suffered, nor does anybody generally become aware of the sin.

Harms of Casting Evil Glances

Shaykh Hakeem Akhtar Sāhib ﷺ has mentioned many harms of casting evil glances in his various books. I will mention some major harms.

1) Disobedience of Allāh ﷻ

Casting evil glances is clearly forbidden by the clear text of the Holy Qur'ān. Allāh ﷻ says,

$$\text{قُلْ لِلْمُؤْمِنِينَ يَغُضُّوا مِنْ أَبْصَارِهِمْ}$$

"Say to the believing men to lower their gazes." (24:30)

The meaning of this verse is to not look at Ghair Mahram women. Therefore, he who casts evil and lustful glances is opposing the clear and explicit command of the Holy Qur'ān and one who opposes the clear and categorical command of the Holy Qur'ān is guilty of perpetrating a Harām act. Thus, to save oneself from this sin, it is sufficient to meditate upon the fact that the one who casts lustful glances, is opposing a commandment of the Holy Qur'ān. In other words, he is disobeying Allāh ﷻ.

2) Breach of Trust

The one who casts evil glances is breaching the trust of Allāh ﷻ. Allāh ﷻ says,

$$\text{يَعْلَمُ خَائِنَةَ الْأَعْيُنِ وَمَا تُخْفِي الصُّدُورُ}$$

"He knows the treachery of the eyes and whatever is concealed by the hearts." (40:19)

Allāh ﷻ uses the word 'Khiyānah' which means to commit mistrust. This indicates that we are not the owners of our eyes, rather, we have been entrusted with them. This is the reason why suicide is forbidden because we are not the owners of our bodies. Allāh ﷻ has entrusted us with our bodies. Since they are a trust from Allāh ﷻ, to use it against His pleasure, to harm it, or to put an end to it is forbidden. If we were the owners of our bodies, then perhaps, we would have the right to use them the way we desire. However, by not giving us the choice and freedom to utilize our bodies the way we desire, is the proof that this is a trust from Allāh ﷻ. To embezzle this trust of Allāh ﷻ is a great crime. The one who casts evil glances is breaching and embezzling the trust of sight which Allāh ﷻ has granted him. The breacher of this trust cannot become the friend of Allāh ﷻ.

3) Curse of the Holy Prophet ﷺ

The one who casts evil glances is cursed by the Holy Prophet ﷺ. The Holy Prophet ﷺ says in a Hadeeth mentioned in Mishkāt;

لَعَنَ اللهُ النَّاظِرَ وَالْمَنْظُوْرَ اِلَيْهِ

"May the curse of Allāh ﷻ be upon the one who casts evil glances and upon the one who presents him/herself to be looked at."

If casting evil glances was a minor sin, then the Holy Prophet ﷺ, being a mercy to mankind, would not have cursed its perpetrator. The curse of the Holy Prophet ﷺ is clear proof that this is a very despicable crime.

4) Weakness of the Heart

By casting evil glances, the thought of that beauty continuously comes into the heart and mind. Through this, the heart is in a continuous struggle and conflict, which causes it to become weak and sick. The curse of casting lustful glances is that along with the eyes, the five senses and the entire body become agitated. In the commentary of the verse:

$$يَعْلَمُ خَائِنَةَ الْأَعْيُنِ وَمَا تُخْفِي الصُّدُورُ$$

"He knows the treachery of the eyes and whatever is concealed by the hearts." (40:19)

Allāma Āloosi ﷺ explains this verse in his Tafseer, Roohul Ma'āni, as follows;

1) Allāh ﷻ is aware of how you turn your eyes around to cast evil glances.

2) The one who casts evil glances uses all five senses. By using the sight, he tries to look at the unlawful beauty. He uses his hearing to listen to her seductive unlawful voice. He uses his lips to try to get an unlawful kiss. Through his touch, he desires to caress the beloved. Through his sense of smell, he wishes to smell the beloved's fragrance.

3) Allāh ﷻ is fully aware of the movements of all the limbs. Allāh ﷻ is watching how a person uses his hands, legs and other limbs in order to obtain his beloved. Whereas, the perpetrator is totally un-

aware that Allāh ﷻ is watching his every move.

4) Allāh ﷻ is fully aware of his final aim, which is fornication or adultery. This is actually an informative sentence that has a warning concealed in it, that is: "I am fully aware of your every move. If you do not abstain, then there will be severe punishment."

Thus, in this verse there is an indication that one will be punished if he does not repent. Casting evil glances is the first stage towards fornication and adultery. This is why Allāh ﷻ forbids the very beginning stage which is casting lustful glances. The example of this sin is like an escalator which automatically takes a person to the final stage, as soon as he puts his feet on the first step. What can be expected of its end result of that action whose beginning is evil, Due to the fact that all the limbs and five senses of the one committing evil glances become agitated and the heart becomes involved in a continuous struggle for a filthy and evil motive, the body and heart of such person becomes weak and sick.

5) Premature Ejaculation

By casting evil glances the sexual desires increase, due to which the heat and temperature of the body rises. This in turn, makes the semen thin and watery due to which a person suffers from premature ejaculation. Such a person is unable to fulfil the rights of his wife properly, due to which their marital relations and eventually their family life is destroyed.

Apart from these harms and dangers, there are many more. I have sufficed on mentioning only five. I hope it will be an eye-opener for every one of us. How can we protect our eyes from lustful glances? What is the prescription which will cure us from this despicable act?

Prescription

I will briefly mention a comprehensive prescription and remedy mentioned by our pious predecessors, which I hope will help us rid ourselves of evil gazes.

1) Salātut-Tawbah (Prayer of Repentance)

Perform two Rakats of Salātut-Tawbah and thereafter, seek forgiveness from Allāh ﷻ for all sins committed. Continue performing Salātut-Tawbah regularly and constantly every night before retiring to bed.

2) Dhikr of Allāh ﷻ

Recite Lāilāha illallāh (there is no god but Allāh ﷻ) 200 times with the thought that, with 'Lā'ilāha' we purify the heart of everyone besides Allāh ﷻ and with 'Illallāh' the love of Allāh ﷻ is entering the heart. Then recite the name of Allāh ﷻ 500 times. When the word Allāh ﷻ emerges from the tongue, imagine the word is also coming from your heart with extreme love and affection.

3) Contemplation Upon the Verse:

$$\text{أَلَمْ يَعْلَمْ بِأَنَّ اللَّهَ يَرَى}$$

"Does he not that know Allāh is watching?" (96:14)

Contemplate (Murāqabah) upon this verse for a few minutes and say to oneself, "Allāh ﷻ is watching me and I am sitting in front of my Creator and Nourisher." Keep praying, "O Allāh ﷻ! Ground this reality in my heart that You are watching me, whereby, I am unable to sin because when this concept and thought is ever present, I will not have the courage to disobey."

4) Contemplation upon Death and the Grave

Reflect upon ones death for a few moments. All your beloved ones including your wife, children, relatives, friends and well-wishers will all bid you farewell. Your clothes will be removed from your body with scissors, you will be bathed, shrouded and taken out of your house forcefully and lowered into a pit. Nobody will stay or aid you now. Only your good deeds will be of any use. The grave is either an orchard from the gardens of Paradise or a pit from the pits of Hell. The four senses through which pleasures were experienced are now dormant. The eyes which feasted upon impermissible beauties are now blind. The ears which listened to music are now deaf. The tongue which tasted a thousand delights is now dumb. Excessive remembrance of death turns the heart away from worldly preoccupations and becomes a means for acquiring the ability (Tawfeeq) to practice good. The Holy Prophet ﷺ said,

"Remember in abundance death, the shatterer of all delights." (Bukhāri)

5) Contemplation upon Resurrection and upon the Punishment of Hell

Thereafter, contemplate for a few minutes upon resurrection, the Day of Judgement and upon standing for account before Allāh ﷻ. Also contemplate upon Hell in such a way as if it is in front of you. Ponder over all the different types of punishments which a person will suffer.

Inshā-Allāh, if we practice upon this prescription, we will be able to safeguard ourselves from immoral gazing. In the beginning, lowering ones gaze will seem very difficult, but by continuous effort, it will gradually become easy.

Shaykh Mufti Taqi Uthmāni Sāhib has described this initial distaste and hardship by means of a parable. In Saudi Arabia, there is a custom to drink small portions of Qahwa (a green tea recipe). When a person experiences the taste for the first time, it appears very unappealing and distasteful. However, thereafter, one becomes so accustomed to Qahwa that just the mere mention of the word or smell pricks the ears and taste buds! Hence, he allegorizes (compares) lowering and protecting ones gaze to the initial bitterness of this drink. It will initially be unappealing, distasteful, difficult and bitter. However, like the drink, repeated striving and lowering the gaze will transform the practice into one of pleasures.

I would like to conclude by mentioning some pearls of wisdom of Sayyidunā Luqmān ﷺ. Sayyidunā Luqmān ﷺ stayed in the company of 4,000 Prophets ﷺ. From the essence of knowledge which he acquired from them, he formulated 6 key points:

1) When in Salāh, protect your heart.
2) When sitting down to eat, protect your throat.
3) When in someone's home, protect your gaze.
4) When in a gathering, protect your tongue.
5) Always remember two things: Allāh ﷻ and death.
6) Always forget two things: forget forever the favours you did for anybody. Secondly, whenever somebody acts inappropriately towards you, then forget it. (Roohul-Ma'āni)

May Allāh ﷻ give us all the Tawfeeq to act upon all the advice mentioned by our pious predecessors.

Āmeen, Yā Rabbal Ālameen.

Other titles from JKN Publications

Your Questions Answered
An outstanding book written by Shaykh Mufti Saiful Islām. A very comprehensive yet simple Fatāwa book and a source of guidance that reaches out to a wider audience i.e. the English speaking Muslims. The reader will benefit from the various answers to questions based on the Laws of Islām relating to the beliefs of Islām, knowledge, Sunnah, pillars of Islām, marriage, divorce and contemporary issues.

UK RRP: £7.90

Hadeeth for Beginners
A concise Hadeeth book with various Ahādeeth that relate to basic Ibādāh and moral etiquettes in Islām accessible to a wider readership. Each Hadeeth has been presented with the Arabic text, its translation and commentary to enlighten the reader, its meaning and application in day-to-day life.

UK RRP: £3.00

Du'ā for Beginners
This book contains basic Du'ās which every Muslim should recite on a daily basis. Highly recommended to young children and adults studying at Islamic schools and Madrasahs so that one may cherish the beautiful treasure of supplications of our beloved Prophet ﷺ in one's daily life, which will ultimately bring peace and happiness in both worlds, Inshā-Allāh.

UK RRP: £2.00

How well do you know Islām?
An exciting educational book which contains 300 multiple questions and answers to help you increase your knowledge on Islām! Ideal for the whole family, especially children and adult students to learn new knowledge in an enjoyable way and cherish the treasures of knowledge that you will acquire from this book. A very beneficial tool for educational syllabus.

UK RRP: £3.00

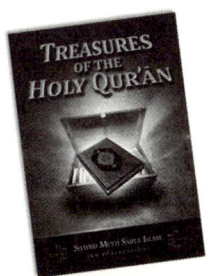

Treasures of the Holy Qur'ān
This book entitled "Treasures of the Holy Qur'ān" has been compiled to create a stronger bond between the Holy Qur'ān and the readers. It mentions the different virtues of Sūrahs and verses from the Holy Qur'ān with the hope that the readers will increase their zeal and enthusiasm to recite and inculcate the teachings of the Holy Qur'ān into their daily lives.

UK RRP: £3.00

Other titles from JKN PUBLICATIONS

Marriage - A Complete Solution
Islām regards marriage as a great act of worship. This book has been designed to provide the fundamental teachings and guidelines of all what relates to the marital life in a simplified English language. It encapsulates in a nutshell all the marriage laws mentioned in many of the main reference books in order to facilitate their understanding and implementation.

UK RRP: £5.00

Pearls of Luqmān
This book is a comprehensive commentary of Sūrah Luqmān, written beautifully by Shaykh Mufti Saiful Islām. It offers the reader with an enquiring mind, Abūndance of advice, guidance, counselling and wisdom.

The reader will be enlightened by many wonderful topics and anecdotes mentioned in this book, which will create a greater understanding of the Holy Qur'ān and its wisdom. The book highlights some of the wise sayings and words of advice Luqmān ملسو هيلع هللا ىلص gave to his son.

UK RRP: £3.00

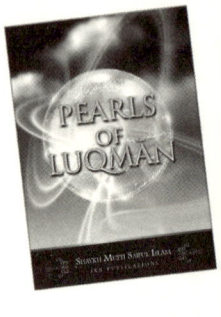

Arabic Grammar for Beginners
This book is a study of Arabic Grammar based on the subject of Nahw (Syntax) in a simplified English format. If a student studies this book thoroughly, he/she will develop a very good foundation in this field, Inshā-Allāh. Many books have been written on this subject in various languages such as Arabic, Persian and Urdu. However, in this day and age there is a growing demand for this subject to be available in English.

UK RRP: £3.00

A Gift to My Youngsters
This treasure filled book, is a collection of Islamic stories, morals and anecdotes from the life of our beloved Prophet ﷺ, his Companions ؓ and the pious predecessors. The stories and anecdotes are based on moral and ethical values, which the reader will enjoy sharing with their peers, friends, families and loved ones.

"A Gift to My Youngsters" – is a wonderful gift presented to the readers personally, by the author himself, especially with the youngsters in mind. He has carefully selected stories and anecdotes containing beautiful morals, lessons and valuable knowledge and wisdom.

UK RRP: £5.00

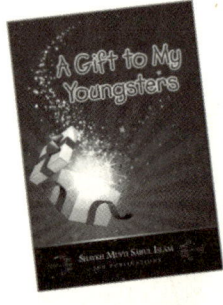

Travel Companion
The beauty of this book is that it enables a person on any journey, small or distant or simply at home, to utilise their spare time to read and benefit from an exciting and vast collection of important and interesting Islamic topics and lessons. Written in simple and easy to read text, this book will immensely benefit both the newly interested person in Islām and the inquiring mind of a student expanding upon their existing knowledge. Inspiring reminders from the Holy Qur'ān and the blessed words of our beloved Prophet ﷺ beautifies each topic and will illuminate the heart of the reader.
UK RRP: £5.00

Pearls of Wisdom
Junaid Baghdādī ؓ once said, "Allāh ﷻ strengthens through these Islamic stories the hearts of His friends, as proven from the Qur'anic verse,
"And all that We narrate unto you of the stories of the Messengers, so as to strengthen through it your heart." (11:120)
Mālik Ibn Dinār ؓ stated that such stories are gifts from Paradise. He also emphasised to narrate these stories as much as possible as they are gems and it is possible that an individual might find a truly rare and invaluable gem among them.
UK RRP: £6.00

Inspirations
This book contains a compilation of selected speeches delivered by Shaykh Mufti Saiful Islām on a variety of topics such as the Holy Qur'ān, Nikāh and eating Halāl. Having previously been compiled in separate booklets, it was decided that the transcripts be gathered together in one book for the benefit of the reader. In addition to this, we have included in this book, further speeches which have not yet been printed.
UK RRP: £6.00

Gift to my Sisters
A thought provoking compilation of very interesting articles including real life stories of pious predecessors, imaginative illustrations and much more. All designed to influence and motivate mothers, sisters, wives and daughters towards an ideal Islamic lifestyle. A lifestyle referred to by our Creator, Allāh ﷻ in the Holy Qur'ān as the means to salvation and ultimate success.
UK RRP: £6.00

Gift to my Brothers
A thought provoking compilation of very interesting articles including real life stories of pious predecessors, imaginative illustrations, medical advices on intoxicants and rehabilitation and much more. All designed to influence and motivate fathers, brothers, husbands and sons towards an ideal Islamic lifestyle. A lifestyle referred to by our Creator, Allāh ﷻ in the Holy Qur'ān as the means to salvation and ultimate success.
UK RRP: £5.00

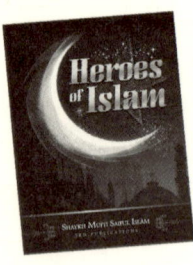

Heroes of Islām
"In the narratives there is certainly a lesson for people of intelligence (understanding)." (12:111)
A fine blend of Islamic personalities who have been recognised for leaving a lasting mark in the hearts and minds of people.
A distinguishing feature of this book is that the author has selected not only some of the most world and historically famous renowned scholars but also these lesser known and a few who have simply left behind a valuable piece of advice to their nearest and dearest. **UK RRP: £5.00**

Ask a Mufti (3 volumes)
Muslims in every generation have confronted different kinds of challenges. Inspite of that, Islām produced such luminary Ulamā who confronted and responded to the challenges of their time to guide the Ummah to the straight path. "Ask A Mufti" is a comprehensive three volume fatwa book, based on the Hanafi School, covering a wide range of topics related to every aspect of human life such as belief, ritual worship, life after death and contemporary legal topics related to purity, commercial transaction, marriage, divorce, food, cosmetic, laws pertaining to women, Islamic medical ethics and much more.
UK RRP: £30.00

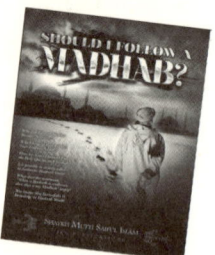

Should I Follow a Madhab?
Taqleed or following one of the four legal schools is not a new phenomenon. Historically, scholars of great calibre and luminaries, each one being a specialist in his own right, were known to have adhered to one of the four legal schools. It is only in the previous century that a minority group emerged advocating a severe ban on following one of the four major schools.
This book endeavours to address the topic of Taqleed and elucidates its importance and necessity in this day and age. It will also, by the Divine Will of Allāh ﷻ dispel some of the confusion surrounding this topic. **UK RRP: £5.00**

Advice for the Students of Knowledge
Allāh ﷻ describes divine knowledge in the Holy Qur'ān as a 'Light'. Amongst the qualities of light are purity and guidance. The Holy Prophet ﷺ has clearly explained this concept in many blessed Ahādeeth and has also taught us many supplications in which we ask for beneficial knowledge.
This book is a golden tool for every sincere student of knowledge wishing to mould his/her character and engrain those correct qualities in order to be worthy of receiving the great gift of Ilm from Allāh ﷻ. **UK RRP: £3.00**

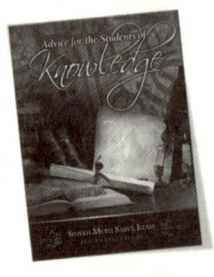

Stories for Children
"Stories for Children" - is a wonderful gift presented to the readers personally, by the author himself, especially with the young children in mind. The stories are based on moral and ethical values, which the reader will enjoy sharing with their peers, friends, families and loved ones. The aim is to present to the children stories and incidents which contain moral lessons, in order to reform and correct their lives, according to the Holy Qur'ān and Sunnah.
UK RRP: £5.00

Pearls from My Shaykh
This book in your hands contains a collection of pearls and inspirational accounts of the Holy Prophet ﷺ, his noble Companions, pious predecessors and some personal accounts and sayings of our well-known contemporary scholar and spiritual guide, Shaykh Mufti Saiful Islām Sāhib. Each anecdote and narrative of the pious predecessors have been written in the way that was narrated by Mufti Saiful Islām Sāhib in his discourses, drawing the specific lessons he intended from telling the story. The accounts from the life of the Shaykh has been compiled by a particular student based on their own experience and personal observation. **UK RRP: £5.00**

Paradise & Hell
This book is a collection of detailed explanation of Paradise and Hell including the state and conditions of its inhabitants. All the details have been taken from various reliable sources. The purpose of its compilation is for the reader to contemplate and appreciate the innumerable favours, rewards, comfort and unlimited luxuries of Paradise and at the same time take heed from the punishment of Hell. Shaykh Mufti Saiful Islām Sāhib has presented this book in a unique format by including the Tafseer and virtues of Sūrah Ar-Rahmān. **UK RRP: £5.00**

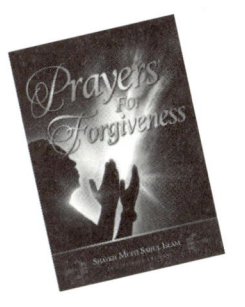

Prayers for Forgiveness
Prayers for Forgiveness' is a short compilation of Du'ās in Arabic, with English translation and transliteration. This book can be studied after 'Du'ā for Beginners' or as a separate book. It includes twenty more Du'ās which have not been mentioned in the previous Du'ā book. It also includes a section of Du'ās from the Holy Qur'ān and a section from the Ahādeeth. The book concludes with a section mentioning the Ninety-Nine Names of Allāh ﷻ with its translation and transliteration. **UK RRP: £3.00**

Scattered Pearls
This book is a collection of scattered pearls taken from books, magazines, emails and WhatsApp messages. These pearls will hopefully increase our knowledge, wisdom and make us realise the purpose of life. In this book, Mufti Sāhib has included messages sent to him from scholars, friends and colleagues which will be beneficial and interesting for our readers Inshā-Allāh. **UK RRP: £4.00**

Poems of Wisdom
This book is a collection of poems from those who contributed to the Al-Mumin Magazine in the poems section. The Hadeeth mentions "Indeed some form of poems are full of wisdom." The themes of each poem vary between, wittiness, thought provocation, moral lessons, emotional to name but a few. The readers will benefit from this immensely and make you ponder over the outlook of life in general.
UK RRP: £4.00